YOU'RE FULL OF IT!

CHANDRA L. BROWN

ACTIVATE PUBLISHING

CINCINNATI, OHIO

Unless otherwise noted, scripture references are from the King James Version of the Bible. Copyright 1972 by Thomas Nelson, Inc.

YOU'RE FULL OF IT! © 2010 by Chandra L. Brown. All rights reserved. Printed in the United States of America. No part of this book may be used or reproduced, scanned or distributed in any printed or electronic form without prior written permission except in the case of reprints in the context of reviews. Please do not participate in or encourage piracy of copyrighted materials in violation of the author's rights. Purchase only authorized editions. For information, address Activate Publishing, P.O. Box 46728 Cincinnati, Ohio 45246-0728 or visit our Web site at www.activatepublishing.com.

Library of Congress Cataloging-in-Publication Data

Brown, Chandra L.
You're Full of It! / Chandra L. Brown.
ISBN 978-0-9846107-2-3
LCCN 2010911793

This publication is designed to provide accurate and authoritative information in regard to the subject matter covered. It is sold with the understanding that neither the author nor the publisher is engaged in rendering legal, investment, accounting, or other professional services. If legal advice or other expert assistance is required, the services of a competent professional should be sought.

ATTENTION: EDUCATIONAL AND PROFESSIONAL ORGANIZATIONS
Activate books are available at quantity discounts with bulk purchase for educational, business, or sales promotional use. Visit www.Yourefullofit.net to schedule the author to speak at your next engagement.

Edited by: Sharon D. Brown
Photography by: Trinity P. Brown

"Embrace, enhance and enjoy all of your spectacular attributes! Always remember and never forget:"

YOU'RE FULL OF IT!

Access workshop dates & Share your thoughts at:
WWW.YOUREFULLOFIT.NET

<u>*Acknowledgments*</u>

To have a partner in life that supports your efforts is a priceless gift. I am fortunate to have that backing from my husband, Donte'.

Donte', your encouragement and belief that I could achieve my dreams even when things looked bleak, means more than you will ever know! You reassured me that everything would be okay in spite of yet another rejection. You were with me in the valley when we did not know our next step and what impact that would have on our family. This served as an indicator of what our relationship is really made of and that it is strong enough to survive the test of time. I know that going through this experience together has strengthened our resolve to overcome in the midst of adverse circumstances.

I don't know if the two of you realize it or not but you inspire mommy daily! Trinity and Christian, you are both such a joy to me! You are a brilliant, caring and loving duo with such an unbelievable sense of humor! Let's keep laughing! You motivate me to move beyond my prior personal best to unchartered areas of myself so that I can model success for you. I want you to know that if mommy can achieve her dreams, so can you. Trinity and Christian, you will do bigger and better things than what mommy accomplished.

Mom, you have been so instrumental in me becoming the person I am today. I admire your spirituality, tenacity, persistence and generous ways. You are unconventional and I absolutely love that about you! I think the fact that I like being unique is one of my better traits. I do not prefer to go along with the status quo just because that is the way something has always been done or that is what is expected. Thank you for passing on your adventurous spirit and love of learning.

Dad, I see more and more of your great qualities in me every day. Thank you for instilling in me the importance of a strong work ethic. I have discovered that I like working with my hands and engaging in problem solving which I owe in large part to you. I always remember you being very dapper, and I attribute my sense of style to you and your insistence on having quality. Mom and Dad, I love and appreciate you more than you will ever know!

Sharifa and Lauren, I love the two of you very much; you both have so much talent! Continue to fulfill your purpose, embrace your greatness and live your life to its fullest!

Bishop Victor Couzens and my Inspirational Baptist Church (IBC) family, thank you for your inspiration, support and prayers! My involvement with the IBC ministry has tremendously blessed my life!

D. T. and cohorts, it is amazing how words of truth at times come from the most unlikely source. When you said, during a meeting, I would thank you for changes you would be making, I thought not likely. To my amazement, in an unexpected way, I am thankful for the decisions that you made. What appeared to be to my detriment resulted in my good ultimately working to my advantage. Thank you for the role you played in my defining moment; here's wishing you all the best!

Contents

Foreword	9
Introduction	12
Stunned	16
Uncertainty	21
Community	31
Activity	36
Revelation	46
Blessed	53
Fulfilled	57
Resourceful	62
Idea	67
Provided	72
Flat	77
Perspective	84
Appreciation	87
Pride	91
Hair	94
Kindred	98
Preparation	102
Receiving	106

Rebranding	112
Networking	117
Words	124
Inspiration	129
Reconnect	132
Connections	139
Feedback	146
Entrepreneur	151
Certification	157
Alumni	161
BNI	165
Authentic	169
Legacy	174
Fitness	180
Impactful	183
How	192
Paradigm	195
Timing	202
Creative	206
Coincidence	209
Choices	213
Finale	216

Foreword

The phrase "You're Full of It" usually has a negative connotation regardless of whether it is used in serious or more lighthearted manner. It usually denotes that someone is full of lies or something else I won't name, but you get the picture! I desired to utilize the shock value of this title to create a shift in thought regarding what one is full of.

The word *full* is loaded with deeper meaning. Personally, I think of *full* as being at capacity whether it is a venue, a gas tank or my stomach after savoring my last piece of red velvet cheesecake! According to the Merriam-Webster thesaurus there are numerous words synonymous with *full* such as maximum, complete, brimming, loaded, packed, overflowing, abounding and top. So when I say "You're Full of It", that means you are complete, brimming over, loaded, and overflowing, but with what? I'll tell you what! So many positive attributes that you may or may not realize you possess such as determination, passion, ideas, and creativity. Many times these qualities are not unearthed until a trial is experienced at some point in life. I want to encourage you that what appears to be an unfortunate circumstance in your life can have a positive outcome.

During times of difficulty, character can be built, patience increased, perseverance mastered, and next steps reassessed. It is amazing how priorities become quite clear because there is a laser sharp focus on what is really important. The trivial falls away and what is left is genuine truth. You are able to see events for what they are without distractions from anyone or anything that does not align with your purpose.

Change for the better sometimes masquerades as adversity. However, if you are able to see beyond the mask, unexpected opportunities can be revealed. My own adversity came in the form of unexpected unemployment but for you it may be a divorce, illness, broken relationship, death or any other situation that leaves you with a sense of loss asking yourself *now what?* I am, by nature, a positive person who views the cup as half full. However, in the face of misfortune, how would I react? What attitude would I display? Well, I can now say I have had the chance to see firsthand how I would react. In *You're Full of It*, I share my journey from how I went from being a successful executive to being unemployed in a matter of hours. Sometimes there is no forewarning before a major life event occurs; it seems as if it appeared out of nowhere. Other times there are signs of what is to come if one will heed them.

I have learned that while one is in the midst of their ordeal, he or she must be honest about what they are feeling. Whether it be anger, hurt, bewilderment or emotional pain, it is crucial to allow these emotions to be felt instead of denying them. This enables truth to be experienced in a deeper way opening up untapped resources from within. Remember, *you're full of it*!

Introduction

The purpose of this book is to let you know that you are not alone. I wrote this book in part to provide practical information regarding how to navigate a crisis situation. Many have found themselves in precarious situations over the past couple of years as a result of the economic downturn and soaring unemployment rates. Although your circumstance might seem insurmountable, it can be overcome!

When you are in the midst of a situation, it can be difficult to view it as temporary or gain a different perspective on what good could result. I am here to encourage you by sharing what helped me to not only survive but come out on the other side of my ordeal with wisdom, a stronger character, sensitivity toward others, and a renewed focus on what is really important in my life. See your trial for what it is -- a test, a time to examine, prove and realize that *you are full of it*! Similar to being in school, you receive feedback on your progress in the form of tests to show your ability in a certain area as well as identify opportunities for improvement. I began to view events that occurred as a test to determine how I would react. I could clearly see how well I was progressing in a given area of my life as well as what I needed to refine. I gained clarity regarding my strengths as well as where I could be stronger.

I began to embrace my journey as a chance to grow, thereby stretching myself, my thinking and my skills. Availing myself to my journey was not always easy. However, I've had so many positive growth experiences I would not have had it any other way. I emphasize that I began to "embrace" my journey not saying that I necessarily "enjoyed" every moment. Gradually I learned to appreciate what my journey was cultivating in me as a woman, wife, mother and daughter. I was able to maintain internal peace that probably would not make sense to someone from the outside. I navigated my days one moment at a time realizing that worry is counterproductive.

My desire was to allow you access to what I experienced from day one of my life taking a very unexpected turn. At times we see a person that has achieved a level of success without knowing the sacrifices that were made. I want you to know that I am similar to you in that I experienced uncertainty as well as "what am I going to do now" moments. However, I made a conscious choice to keep moving forward gaining strength from a belief that my life would improve. I choose to view my circumstances through that filter. My belief was activated by the following principles: *you have what you say, thoughts and words are powerful helping to create your destiny* as well as *give and you shall receive* among many others.

    I became focused on having a clear vision for my life and my family to ensure being on the right path to fulfill our purpose. Leaving a legacy became a top priority for me. I desired to model for my children that events in our lives are not just about me or our family, but impact our community-at-large. Therefore, I could not afford to engage in a continuous pity party, but had to pull myself together by being focused, disciplined and consistent in how I lived my life on a daily basis. The "Wisdom Won," sections at the end of each chapter are my take on the lessons I have learned and that I believe will be helpful for others. According to Proverbs 4:7, "Wisdom is the principal thing; therefore get wisdom and with all thy getting get understanding". I perceive this as meaning it is important to be smart and have strong intellect, but gaining wisdom is the real priority. Wisdom is defined in many ways. I especially like a definition from webdictionary.co.uk that states wisdom is the ability to *apply* and *utilize* knowledge with common sense and insight. Merriam-Webster provides wonderful synonyms for wisdom such as discernment, perception, and comprehension to name a few. I attached the word 'won' to 'wisdom' because I view conquering a trial as winning!

      Similar to how studying increases one's chance of receiving a passing grade, practicing a desired skill increases the chances of winning in that area. Merriam-webster.com defines win as "to achieve victory." The joint phrase *Wisdom Won* can be translated as applied knowledge that leads to victory! So, knowledge that is earned or won through one's trials is not easily defeated!

Stunned

I returned to work from Subway with a salad for lunch that I planned to eat in my office. On the way to my office I stopped to mention an idea to one of my employees. In that same moment, the person whom I reported to put his hand on my shoulder and asked that I come with him into the conference room. I did not even stop to put my salad down. I followed him into the conference room where sat a Human Resource (HR) representative. I walked in and sat down. My mind was swirling with questions, the main one being what is going on? Little did I know how odd this meeting was about to become.

The person to whom I reported told me in a cold, very matter of fact manner that my position was eliminated and that the HR person would explain the rest. He said nothing else to me but directed my attention to the HR person who shared additional details. I was escorted from the conference room to my office with my salad in hand. I was informed to either pack up my office immediately or return later. I decided to collect my belongings immediately.

The HR representative located boxes for me to utilize and instructed a separate individual to monitor my progress. As I packed, the person to whom I reported paced back and forth in front of my office searching for my colleague. Unbeknownst to me at the time, his position was eliminated as well. My office was personalized, therefore, I had pictures to remove from the walls, awards, training materials and other items accumulated over a two year period. I was provided two small boxes that were quickly filled to capacity. The HR representative searched for additional boxes and plastic bags that I could use to transport my possessions.

The realization of what was happening sunk in causing hot tears to stream down my face. The HR representative inquired whether I wanted to come back later and I replied, "No I will collect my property now." Employees from other departments entered my office to hug me as well as say good-bye. My departure became quite an emotional scene. I carried a box out to my car that was parked in the employee lot. I drove my car to the front lot so that it would be easier to load my now "boxed up" office.

A fire exit near my office provided easier access to load my car. The fire alarm was temporarily disabled allowing me to load my car with the remaining boxes. My car was completely full -- the trunk, the back seat, and the passenger seat were bulging with my belongings. The alarm on the emergency exit reset causing the alarm to activate as if to announce Chandra Brown is vacating the building permanently. I was finally down to my last box, therefore I went out to where my team was sitting to give them hugs as well as tell them I enjoyed working with them and to keep doing their best.

 I loaded my final box, then drove from the parking lot in a stunned fog. It was a beautiful sunny day in July; however, it was hard for me to focus on that fact because I was in a state of shock. I called my husband, to tell him what had transpired, but kept getting his voicemail. I called my children's daycare provider telling her in a quivering voice that I had just experienced a change in my job status which meant our children would no longer be coming. She showed a great deal of generosity by waiving the withdrawal fees associated with removing our children without notice. I appreciated her sensitivity so much that I pledged when I was in a position to do so, I would pay her the fees.

Before I realized, I arrived at home by driving on auto pilot. I exited my car then observed all of my possessions that one hour earlier were displayed in my office. As I placed my work Blackberry on my desk, prior to leaving, an HR representative told me to take it with me in case there was information that I needed since it was hard to think straight in the current situation. I followed the recommendation regarding my Blackberry. I attempted to use my Blackberry when I arrived home, but evidently soon after I exited the building, all of my access was removed as if I never existed. My position was not eliminated for performance reasons but that was not evident by how events unfolded that afternoon. I began unloading all of the bags and boxes into my kitchen. Then I sat down, took in the surreal scene while contemplating all that had transpired as I finally had an opportunity to . . . enjoy my salad.

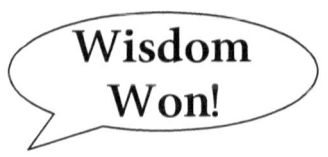

I was provided information that indicated that my job might be eliminated; however, I received no official statement at that time.
If you receive informal information that may affect you, take the necessary precautions to ensure your affairs are in order. That is not the time to be in denial but it is the moment to prepare for various scenarios and outcomes. I believe events happen for a reason and many times we receive forewarning if the signals are heeded.

I went from being a successful executive to an unemployed individual in a matter of minutes.
This fact demonstrates how important it is not to connect your identity to a job position, marital status, financial standing or any other external identifier because circumstances can change quickly. This made me assess my self-image focusing on the quality of person that I am -- independent of what I do or what has been done to me.

Be sensitive to what others are experiencing and, where feasible, help ease their burden.
My children's sitter showed me a kindness that I sincerely appreciated. It may seem like a small gesture, but her waiving the early withdrawal fee assisted me financially. Her actions also conveyed generosity and genuine concern when I needed it most.

Uncertainty

I revealed what happened to me because I desire to be transparent so that you can understand the range of emotions that are involved in such a situation. Whether your circumstance was similar or different, there are probably emotions that were evoked to which you could relate. These feelings include, but are not limited to, anger, confusion, hurt, and bewilderment. Then there are the questions, "what is my next step?" and "how do I navigate this road I've never travelled?"

My daughter's birthday was 5 days after my job was eliminated. The invitations had already been sent. Additionally, I wanted to maintain a sense of normalcy since I had already withdrawn my children from their summer program. At the same time, I was contemplating where I could reduce our spending since our financial future was uncertain.

Being unemployed allowed me to empathize with other individuals in the same position. I have discovered so much about myself throughout this process. I realize now, more than ever, that what I experience is not only about me. I am intertwined with people in ways that I am aware of as well as some that are not as obvious.

It was difficult for me to verbalize that I was unemployed. Over time my job title had become my placeholder. Without my title I felt peculiar as if I did not belong. I utilized creative means to state that I was unemployed such as I am between opportunities, I am in transition, or I am the former Director of Internal Audit at ABC Company. The reason it was so excruciating for me to come to terms with being unemployed was because I had never experienced this previously. I have worked at various companies since I was 15 leaving positions on my own terms either due to better opportunities or career advancement. It seemed to me that I lacked the control I normally wielded over my destiny.

Mary, a Life Coach in my Toastmaster group, delivered a powerful speech that was immensely helpful for me. She stated that an event has no meaning until we bring meaning to it. One of her examples was very appropriate for me because it dealt with job loss. She explained that in its purest sense a job elimination is a neutral event until we start adding our own meaning to it. One person's response might be, "what am I going to do?!" Their prior experience might equate not having a job to being catastrophic. This person may recall how her father's job loss resulted in worry and uncertainty. So her response might be, "how am I going to pay my mortgage and my children's tuition?" Whereas another person might have viewed the scenario as opening a door to something better. This second person might remember when his mother lost her job it resulted in her receiving a new opportunity that did not require travel; in addition, she was paid a higher salary. His response might be framed as, "let's see how we can make our circumstances work."

Now, do not misunderstand. I am in no way diminishing the first response because that was me. However, I gradually moved into a mindset of "okay this is where we are – how can we make this work?" It may sound cliché but dealing with life's issues is really about being receptive to new choices as well as viewing life with a fresh perceptive. My life had gone in a completely different direction than what I anticipated, but in a good way. I believe certain opportunities surfaced in my life due, in large part, to my being open to change.

Availing yourself to change is vital because the plans you have for your life can be altered in an instant. My position as the Director of Internal Audit was eliminated on Tuesday July 15, 2008. I was scheduled to fly to San Francisco that upcoming Sunday for Stephen Covey's Great Leaders, Great Teams, and Great Results training from July 21-24. All of the arrangements were made but those plans were altered just like everything else. In hindsight, my not attending the training worked out for me because my daughter's birthday was on July 20, and I was concerned about flying out on her birthday thereby reducing our time together. With this new development regarding my job status, that was no longer a concern!

Instead I woke up on Wednesday, July 16, 2008 with the realization that I did not have to go to work because I was off; more specifically I couldn't go to work due to no longer having a job. Similar to many people I relished vacation days and having time off, but not like this. Time off is not enjoyable when you have the anxiety of *what am I going to do for income* hanging over your head. At various points in my career, I have received stellar training on a variety of topics. However, I never obtained guidance on how to exit a company as a result of a layoff, job elimination, or other unexpected circumstances. This was all unchartered territory for me.

    The day following my job elimination, my internal clock woke me up at 5:00 a.m., the time I would normally begin preparing for work. I felt the need to spend time in peaceful thought before my family awoke. I had not been engaging in quiet time in the morning to obtain a clear path for my day, erroneously thinking that I did not have enough time. Now, all I have is time. I sought God for direction and guidance so that my steps would be ordered. My husband, Donte', took a vacation day the day following my job elimination - sleeping most of the morning. I have noticed, over the years, that when he feels stressed he becomes withdrawn to process his thoughts. He desired to demonstrate his support for me; however, he did not know what to do or say. I quickly realized that spouses are affected as well by such a sudden and significant change. My husband's behavior served as a reminder that people need to process change in their own way. I want to publicly acknowledge my husband, Donte', for his strength and support in the face of so many unknowns. For those of you with significant others navigating an uncertain journey with you, make an effort to understand what he or she is enduring.

Midday on July 16, I received a voicemail from a friend informing me about a Career Fair being held in downtown Cincinnati. Then an acquaintance who was in the midst of a career transition called telling me she was attending the same Career Fair. I thought hearing the same information from two different individuals was confirmation that I should attend as well. I put on a pant suit, styled my hair, printed my resume and headed to the Career Fair. Donte' taking the day off worked to our benefit because he stayed with our children while I was away.

When I arrived at the career fair, I quickly discovered that the majority of positions were entry level. However, experiencing the Career Fair was a good eye opener for me. It was extremely humbling to state, "I am looking for a job." This personal reality check allowed me to relate to others that found themselves in similar situations. When I arrived home, Trinity and Christian were waiting to learn whether I obtained a job. I informed them not yet.

My job loss and subsequent reduction in income translated into a teachable moment for our children. I openly shared with them how some of our prior practices would be altered. For example, we were in the habit of having dinner at various restaurants every Friday evening. Going out to dinner was fun; however, it had become a set expectation instead of being viewed as a privilege that was genuinely appreciated. Dining out was scaled back drastically, but when we did indulge we were creative with coupons instituting the sharing of sides instead of each family member having their own duplicate items. Our modifications provided our children with a reality check which resulted in them being thankful for any nonessentials we were able to do. Truthfully, "extras" had become so commonplace in our home that we were all better able to decipher between a true necessity versus a want.

I received an e-mail from a prior colleague inquiring about how I was handling my job elimination. He asked had I heard from my employees and I replied no. The realization that I had not heard from my team made me a bit sad as though I was not appreciated. I encouraged myself that the people who matter in my life care about me. My personal pep talk took some time to sink in but eventually I felt better. Something else that has made me feel good was jumpstarting my day on the treadmill while listening to my Bible Experience CD's. I got up to 8,000 steps on the treadmill before even walking throughout the day; I was sure to reach the recommended goal of 10,000 steps a day!

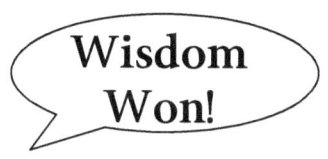

View events as neutral being aware of the meaning you assign to a given event based on your prior experiences or beliefs.
It is vital to discern why you are viewing an event a certain way and why people offer the advice they offer. Third parties might derive meaning based on their personal bias or limited perspective. Ensure that you encourage yourself as well as receive support from positive people that maintain an attitude of *how can we make this happen?*

Those close to you can also be deeply affected by changes in your life.
I think we intuitively realize this is true; however, we need to explicitly communicate appreciation for their patience and understanding. Ensure that you take into consideration the feelings of the important people in your life remembering that support should flow in all directions.

During the midst of a crisis, character is built as well as empathy for mankind. Merriam-webster.com describes character as the standard of right and wrong, overall quality of your reputation and what makes us individuals setting us apart from others.
Conquering an issue makes one capable of clarifying for themselves the important principles in their life instead of relying on what others think or say. Credibility is earned as well because the individual

knows whereof they speak due to the issue they endured. Handling an ordeal enables one to more directly empathize with others in a way that would not be possible had the situation not been encountered firsthand.

Community

    My children wanted to play at our local park so off we went. I allowed them to remain in the water area as long as they wanted without our usual rush. I brought my business contacts along so I could call them to make them aware that I was actively looking for my next opportunity.

    Since my mom was on vacation, this was my first chance to talk with her concerning the events that had transpired over the prior two days. On this particular day, she was on a layover at the Chicago airport so we both had time to chat. I shared with her all of the details about my job elimination along with how that left me feeling. As always, she was very encouraging. She confirmed for me that when one door closes another one opens. Intuitively, I knew this was true, but now I have firsthand experience to determine if I *believed* it for myself.

    Trinity and Christian moved from the water park to the regular activity side after enjoying an ice cream cone. I located a bench while my children continued to play. I spotted a woman I knew, as

Joshua's mom, from my children's school. I said good-bye to my mom then struck up a conversation with Joshua's mom who sat down on the bench next to me. I asked how her summer was going; then she inquired whether I had taken a vacation day. I informed her that my job was eliminated 2 days prior. She commented that unemployment was beginning to increase. She shared how she was somewhat at a crossroads herself.

As we began discussing her occupation, I learned that she was a Human Resource recruiter. Our discussion would not have been as enriching if I had held the conversation at a surface level, glossing over why I was able to be at the park in the middle of the day. God's timing is awesome! What are the chances that we would both be at the same park at the same time when that was not part of our normal routine. Our paths have crossed numerous times before; however, I never made an opportunity to become better acquainted. Joshua's Mom began listing the executive recruiting firms in our city that I was not aware of previously.

In that moment, God showed me clearly that my situation was not just about me. Another mom sat down next to me on the park bench. After a few moments, she stated that she overheard part of our conversation then began sharing how she was laid-off from her job the prior week. She said she was sitting at home feeling depressed when the thought came to mind that she should go to the park to let her children play. The three of us meeting that afternoon was divine destiny. Due to each of us experiencing similar challenges, we were able to serve as encouragement for each other. Throughout our conversation, I was trying to remember Joshua's mom's name to no avail. However, as we were leaving we both re-introduced ourselves and I learned that her name was April. God is faithful in providing me with periodic signs that everything is working together for my good!

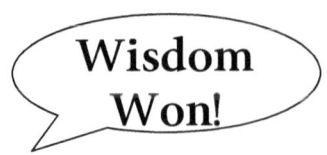

I learned the importance of being transparent and genuine. It is vital to obtain depth in conversations moving beyond surface level chat. At times, it is appropriate to express your vulnerabilities as well as your strengths. In many instances, people are willing to assist if they are aware that you need help.

When faced with the option of being authentic or glossing over what events are transpiring in your life, be authentic. Especially if someone specifically asks how you are doing. Sharing what you are experiencing can result in you being helped as well as others by confirming they are not alone in their circumstance.

Become better acquainted with individuals that you come in contact with on a regular basis. It is amazing how we encounter people in passing without learning what they do for a living, what they have going on in their lives, or what they have as passions or interests.

I have discovered that most people are willing to share information about themselves if asked. Certain information may not be offered without prompting with open-ended question such as, "What would you like to be doing?" Then when the person responds, listen with genuine interest along with a thought of how you can help him further his pursuits.

Enduring adversity is not just about me, but, in time, will serve as an encouragement to others. Frequently, you cannot wait until your storm is over before comforting someone else.

You may think, "How can I tell someone that things are going to get better when I am currently in the same or similar situation?" You are able to offer that optimism due to being uniquely qualified. Due to having experienced a similar circumstance, you understand what emotions are present, and you can offer a level of strength that someone else may not have attained.

Activity

My husband and I discussed our next steps regarding my job search, our family finances and various other topics that needed to be addressed. As a result of this conversation, he thought it would be beneficial for me to spend the remainder of the summer with our children then be prepared to begin a new job in the fall when they returned to school. Therefore, my plan of action was actively seeking an opportunity with the anticipation of a start date that coincided with my children's return to school.

On the morning of Thursday July 17, I received an e-mail from Flex jobs. I applied for a Strategic Director position that would allow me to work from home. I was excited to take the next steps with that opportunity.

On Friday, July 18, I received an e-mail from Teach America that a writing sample and PowerPoint presentation were required to complete my application; I transmitted the requested items. April e-mailed me a variety of employment resources. I thank God for her generosity in sharing information.

I will seek an opportunity to be a blessing in her life as well. I will not forget her kindness!

A point of inspiration that propelled me forward was talking to Vickie, a colleague from a previous employer. I actually took notes from our conversation to capture the words of wisdom she was sharing so I could refer to them later. She is in the midst of her own journey of trusting in God along with seeking what He wants her to do with her life. Being contacted by three of my employees was uplifting as well.

On Monday July 21, I met with Tracy a local executive recruiter. During our conversation, she mentioned BNI which I later learned was the acronym for Business Networking International. I researched BNI on the internet discovering that it appeared to be an awesome networking organization. I was thankful that my knowledge base of available resources was expanding. I was scheduled to meet with Kim from another executive recruiting firm on Thursday, July 24. However, since I was near her office I called to inquire whether I could move my appointment. It pays to ask because she was agreeable to altering my appointment which resulted in me saving gas and time.

On Wednesday, July 23, I applied to a local company for the positions of Senior Internal Audit Manager as well as Senior Business Consultant. Both opportunities were a great fit for my background and experience. I received an e-mail from an HR representative expressing an interest in discussing the opportunities with me.

I am eternally grateful to the countless individuals who assisted me with my networking efforts. While I cannot name each person, I will name one that serves as a representation of the rest. A prior colleague invited my husband and I to her home where I met some wonderful people. One person that I met was Shawnda. After the two of us spoke briefly, she told me to forward my resume to her so that she could distribute it to a larger group of people. I thought I *knew* how to network; however, I experienced an epiphany in that moment that I could improve in that area.

I am so thankful for the favor God has given me with various individuals as well as showing me how I should respond in turn. Although I viewed myself as a helpful person, I have acquired a new level of sensitivity. Instead of telling someone, "if I hear of an opportunity, I will let you know." I take a more personal interest. Then, if possible, I speak to others on the person's behalf or at a minimum forward their resume to a hiring manager. I have a greater focus on demonstrating empathy by genuinely supporting someone's efforts instead of just saying I'll keep you in mind. I decided within myself that when I was in a position to do so, I would proactively help others who were in transition or needed assistance navigating next steps.

On Friday, July 25, I connected with the HR representative from the local firm where I applied for a Senior Audit Manager position. We scheduled a phone interview for Monday, July 28 at 10:30 a.m. I prayed to God that I would have favor then thanked Him in advance for my having an outstanding face to face interview.

On Saturday, July 26, April e-mailed me an invitation to an executive networking meeting to be held on August 6. I registered for the meeting knowing that now, more than ever, I have to tangibly show my appreciation to April.

I paid our household bills then deposited the check I received in lieu of being able to provide two weeks along with the regular pay for my last 80 hours worked. I am living by faith, because I moved forward with paying the first tuition payment for my children's school. I do not know what the future holds, but I believe God will honor my faith.

Whenever I questioned God about not receiving a job offer or what we were supposed to do to supplement our income, I felt Him speak to my heart. He told me, "I want you to trust me. You have a relationship with me. What are you lacking?" When I thought about it, there was nothing that my family really needed.

On Monday, July 28, I filed for unemployment benefits online. I learned that it is vital to file for unemployment as soon as a job terminates for an eligible reason. I had no prior exposure to obtaining unemployment and did not know that one could not retroactively receive benefits for the time unemployed prior to filing. I originally thought I was disallowed two weeks of unemployment benefits. Even though I was not given the opportunity to provide two weeks' notice, fortunately I was paid for that time.

I e-mailed my resume to yet another recruiter. I then received a call from a different recruiter who learned that my position was eliminated by talking to one of my prior employees. Also, I completed the phone screening for the Senior Audit Manager position. The salary was less than anticipated; however, I was still interested in pursuing an on-site interview. The recruiter stated that they were at the beginning stages of the hiring process and would begin interviews in two weeks.

I received an e-mail from Teach for America that they were no longer considering me as a candidate. Tuesday, July 29, I decided along with pursuing corporate opportunities I would endeavor to obtain consulting work on my own. I conducted research on grants for women business owners and called my contact from a grant writing course I attended. I began working on a business plan for my venture. I spoke with Al from the grant writing course I had attended a few months prior, and he provided me with good insights.

I also spoke with a colleague from a prior employer. She called to make me aware that she was relocating and that her position would be available. She indicated that it might be beneficial to contact the Director of Audit, who was my previous boss, regarding this opening. I called my prior boss and he indicated there were no openings in Internal Audit at my level, but he would inquire within other departments on my behalf. I was able to make peace with my old boss regarding leaving my previous position without disclosing my new employer in order to be discreet about my new opportunity. I felt relieved and humbled to have this conversation with him and obtain his forgiveness.

In the midst of all I was doing, I quickly learned that looking for your next opportunity is a full-time job in and of itself. It amazed me how the flurry of activity at the onset of my job search has slowed to a crawl. The time I have spent alone allowed me to reflect, assess, and decide what I wanted next for my life. A dear friend called and told me she thought about me during her quiet time. She wanted me to know that this was a time of rest and preparation for me. I thought about what she expressed to me and really took it to heart. I found that I was still quite busy even though I was no longer working outside of my home. I realized that prior to my job elimination my life was a blur with me rushing from one obligation to the next. Now, I have a better appreciation for my time valuing it as a precious gift.

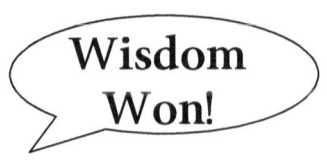

Commit to giving your best effort in whatever opportunity you are pursuing while at the same time be able to accept rejection with grace.
For each job opportunity I sought, I expended a lot of time and effort to comprehensively fill out online applications, customize my resume to the particular position, convey the reason I was looking, and provide my work experience multiple times. I worked diligently to maintain excellence throughout every stage of the process. It was disappointing to learn that a company was going in a different direction, but I moved forward not allowing myself to remain discouraged.

Provide the level of assistance you would want to obtain if you were to find yourself on the receiving end.
Being on the receiving end of genuine help allowed me to better understand how to provide proactive assistance. Shawnda may never realize the hope she ignited within me that night by displaying her sincere interest in my situation by promptly helping me in the following days. I will remember as well as emulate her generosity and kindness.

View a time of transition as an opportunity instead of a detriment. I've had some of my clearest thoughts once I became quiet and still shutting out all outside interference.

I had no choice but to slow down which I later found was really needed. I discovered I was going through the motions; existing but not truly living. I was constantly in turmoil because of an inner conflict between what I wanted my life to be and the reality of what it was day in and day out. Take time to reevaluate and reassess the direction, fullness and purpose of your life.

Revelation

I continued to submit my resume each week for various job applications engaging in multiple conversations with numerous recruiters to no avail. During this time, I watched Bishop T.D. Jakes *Reposition Yourself* DVD series. I also read Dr. Myles Munroe's books on Vision and Leadership, titled, "The Principles and Power of Vision" and "The Spirit of Leadership" respectively. I also read "Hinds Feet on High Places" by Hannah Hunnard. The information I learned as well as inspiration I received from each of the resources was immense! It seemed as if my awareness was somewhat obstructed before being exposed to the principles in those materials. Afterwards, I operated in a more conscious and deliberate manner. I began to live my life on purpose, not just by random happenstance.

On Sunday, August 10, my family attended church where we heard a motivating sermon. A conversation with friends, the Friday night prior, contained common themes from the sermon that was preached on Sunday. The message involved worshipping God, remaining humble, and being immersed in God's word. I realized that I must stay connected to God to hear from Him. If a close friend calls me on the phone, I know who it is because I recognize their voice. I am honing my relationship with God so that I have that same familiarity with Him.

Reading the Bible beginning at Genesis is an undertaking I had never attempted. As I studied the passages in Genesis, the words seemed to come alive revealing clarity for my situation. In times of trouble, many people cling to their faith receiving inner strength to endure and conquer their circumstances. I desired to hear clearly from God regarding my next steps. As I read the Old Testament, I felt compelled to highlight the instances when God spoke thereby identifying what He stated focusing on the situation being addressed in each verse. I observed where God spoke in terms of covenants. I felt as though Joshua chapter 1 had some points that were applicable to my life. Particularly, Joshua 1 verses 11 and 15 where God instructs Joshua that the land on the other side of Jordan was his, but he had to possess it.

I felt as though I came out of my own personal "Egypt" and was being positioned to possess everything that God had for me. I felt like God was telling me directly through these scriptures that I can have what I desire as long as it aligns with His will. However, my dreams and aspirations were not going to fall in my lap; I had to fight for them!

Friends, colleagues, relatives and others may categorize you based on their skewed or narrow perspective of your prior actions or achievements. Frequently, how you are viewed is based on what others have witnessed to date. Personally, individuals in my life know that I have an Accounting degree and have worked in Internal Audit for years. Naturally, that is how they view me. However, as I began to discover untapped skills and abilities I possessed, but did not necessarily display to others, I saw myself from a broader perspective.

I had to alter my own mindset to see myself in a different light. I realized that I had a narrow perception of myself that prevented me from achieving things outside that realm. I began writing, built a website and strived to hone other skills as well. I was undergoing an internal transformation that was not visible to the natural eye but was nonetheless resulting in positive changes. I was less affected by trivial items becoming more passionate about fulfilling my purpose in life.

All of my formal education and training has benefited me tremendous. I am grateful that I was able to obtain postsecondary level education gaining so much in my life due to my education. I now see myself using that education and training in more unconventional ways. Instead of operating in purely an accounting arena I have been using my leadership, organization and critical thinking skill sets, along with others, in different ways. For so long I felt as though I was not achieving what I was destined to attain. Although I was not fulfilled in my daily work activities, I continued to excel so I persisted.

Eventually, through my job elimination, I was forced to confront the fact that I was not fulfilled. I knew I was not operating in my passion and purpose. I began to pay attention to what activities in my life brought me fulfillment. As I spent time alone contemplating my next steps, clarity was revealed. It was time for me to use my gifts and talents to achieve what I am meant to do, not just what I am capable of accomplishing!

I applied for an Adjunct Faculty opportunity with a well-respected university; however, the interview would not occur for nearly two months. I placed the date on my calendar while I continued to seek other career opportunities as well as entrepreneurial endeavors. From the outside looking in, my circumstances probably appeared the same. However, there was a change occurring on the inside of me. I felt a peace about our situation that could only be explained by the fact I knew God was in control. I recommitted my life to glorifying Him knowing He would provide for my family.

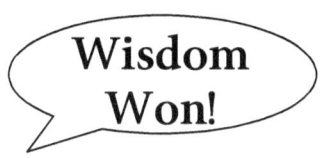

Continue to expand your horizons by broadening your perspective with positive as well as practical information. Stimulate your mind and remain motivated.

Although reading is an activity I always enjoyed, it became extremely beneficial for me during my time of transition. Your diversion might be reading, a pottery class, or even projects around your home. A form of recreation aids in sustaining your sense of self worth as well as feeling of achievement as you complete a project or learn a new concept.

Establishing a spiritual foundation builds inner strength helping to reduce stress due to reliance on a power greater than one's self.

Remaining connected to God yields clear direction for next steps. My method of staying in relationship with God and discerning His will for my life came from reading my Bible, spending time with Him first thing in the morning and following biblical principles.

Press forward instead of dwelling on the past which does nothing but impede your momentum and growth.

I came to terms with my current situation, acknowledged accomplishments from the past and looked forward to what I was endeavoring to achieve in my future. Once I began focusing on moving forward, instead of expending my energy on looking back, I had an unexplainable peace about our situation. Our circumstances had not changed, but my outlook had and that made all the difference.

Blessed

My mom invited me to attend a day long retreat titled, "A Day of Refreshing". The retreat location was a beautiful place to engage in a day of reflection. I benefitted tremendously from the change of scenery and a time specifically set aside for me to surround myself with peace and tranquility. Initially, all the participants met together as a group, eventually being instructed to find a place on the property to meditate, contemplate or just relax. The weather was picture perfect with the sun shining brightly, the birds chirping and a light breeze prancing between the trees. The setting was extremely peaceful.

Alone with my thoughts, I wrote responses in my journal to the prompting questions provided by the facilitator that related to our direction in life. The theme for the day was *blessings* in terms of what the word means and how do we bless God. While I was intrigued by the idea of blessing God, this notion seemed to be in alignment with a different concept I had recently heard. The sermon about 'being broken' focused on how Jesus took bread, blessed it, broke it, and then gave it to his disciples to eat. Jesus does the same thing with us as far as blessing us, breaking us and then and only then are we ready to be served up to the world, to serve the world fulfilling our God given purpose. This lesson profoundly changed the way I viewed my circumstances. This insight gave me hope that everything I was experiencing was occurring for a greater purpose that would ultimately work for my good and the good of others.

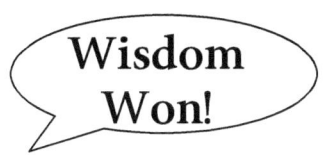

Set aside a time of quiet reflection. It is imperative to be comfortable with your own thoughts. I know that spending time inside your head without any television, music, etc...is a frightening aspect to some people, but to effectively interact with others in your life you have to reach a level of contentment with yourself.

I have lived with internal conflict for a while. The life I envisioned for myself versus the life I was actually living did not align. If you find you are not where you want to be in life, this is the time to take action addressing obstacles that are blocking your achievement. This could also be the time to enlist and accept support from those individuals that have your best interest at heart.

Documenting your thoughts, ideas, and desires has a way of bringing your emotions to the forefront where they can be addressed. Writing can be described as verbalizing in silence. You hear your own voice as you express yourself in writing. Journaling provided me with a record of events, a measure of my progress, a release of negative emotions, and so much more. It could tremendously benefit you to maintain a journal for yourself and bestow them as presents. Journals are truly a gift that continues to give.

Preparation for your destiny comes in various forms. Cautiously view your circumstances in the correct context. What may appear detrimental could work for your ultimate good.

A huge factor in my walking into my own personal destiny was being humbled to the point that I had a renewed empathy and desire to serve others through my life.

Fulfilled

My husband and I were talking one evening when he inquired about whether I would be interested in teaching. He also made the comment that he did not expect me to make the same salary I had previously earned. He expressed that it would be great to have that same income; however, as long as we could maintain our household he was satisfied. I shared with him how much I appreciated him verbalizing his thoughts. His sentiments released me from pressure and stress I did not realize I harbored until I felt a deep sense of relief from his words.

As the spouse of a person in transition, you wield power to encourage or discourage through explicit sentiments or omission of opinions that could be misconstrued. During October, I applied for faculty positions at all of the local colleges and universities. My job search extended into the holiday season with no job offers in sight. Additionally, I was not receiving any responses on my job applications. I prepared for the university interview that initially seemed so far in the future but arrived with me still actively looking for a full-time opportunity.

During November, 2008 Jason from a well respected university interviewed me. The principles of the university aligned with my personal philosophy. Excitement coursed through me even though the opportunity was part-time. I have always envisioned myself teaching at some point in my life. Imagine my dismay when the interviewer expressed concern about me being unemployed at the time of the interview. I understood his thought process about how my being unemployed could present a credibility issue with the students; however, I was deflated by the expectation of already holding a position to obtain employment.

I thought being in transition offered valuable insights. There is much discussion about one being prepared to enter a new position. Individuals are educated on how to generate a stellar resume as well exude confidence during an interview. These aforementioned skills and many others are necessary; however, I also see the need for discussions about exiting a job with grace and not tying one's identity to a job or title. I was elated when I was selected to continue on in the candidate evaluation process. I was afforded the opportunity to become part of the university family. I enjoy teaching tremendously.

Explicitly communicate to people dear to you how you perceive your current condition. A deeper understanding can be gained as well as generating support and encouragement.

I felt liberated to hear my husband's expectation about any future job I obtained. Since we never explicitly discussed our views in this manner, I took the stance that my prior salary was anticipated. My husband's specific communication ushered in an amazing transformation within me as well as our relationship.

Attempt a new pursuit utilizing your current skills in a new manner.

Teaching became a full circle moment for me. Inherently, I am an educator in my personal life as well as my professional pursuits. While employed in corporate America, I consistently worked to hone skill sets, thinking critically and enhance leadership skills for myself as well as my employees. I was able to transfer those skills into a new career path. Explore skill sets you possess but have not utilized in a specific manner; this alternate use might be the catalyst for your next phase in life.

Once you are given the opportunity you desired, cherish it. Demonstrate your gratitude by displaying excellence in all of your actions.

When I learned that I would be teaching, I was ecstatic and extremely appreciative. I committed to impart my absolute best to my students.

Resourceful

I have decided to embrace my journey. I am not alleging that I do not encounter difficult moments; however, I concentrated on appreciating each step although I could not see the entire picture. I have become extremely resourceful as a result of my transition. My cell phone bill charges were $100 plus a month due to having unlimited minutes as well as other features. I scaled down to a basic plan returning to my former intent of utilizing my cell phone for emergencies. I simply requested for people to contact me at my home number. I know this type of modification is not feasible for everybody; however, it has been successful for me particularly with my desire to decrease expenses. My monthly phone bill was reduced by a resounding 50% a month.

I strived to maintain extracurricular activities as an integral part of my life. I discovered free salsa dance instruction was held every Thursday night on Fountain Square in downtown Cincinnati during the summer months. I decided to partake in the festivities and invited a girlfriend to join me. Remain active by not permitting yourself to withdraw from family & friends; doing so can result in missing out on enjoyable events.

Shift your focus onto whatever positives are occurring in your life. This in no way dismisses issues that need to be addressed; however, do not expend all of your energy handling predicaments. Recall that your career, relationships and unexpected events are only one aspect of your life. They do not define your total person.

I received a call from a prior employee as we travelled to salsa dancing; she was encouraging by telling me she missed me and wanted to keep in touch. In that moment, I realized how traumatic my job elimination had been for my staff leaving them not knowing what to say or how to react.

Not fully understanding the ramifications of my job elimination, our children still desired to go to Kings Island as we have in the past. However, this was an expensive proposition at a time that we were determining the best use of our funds. I conducted research on the Internet to locate Kings Island coupons; my efforts resulted in a promotion titled, The Twilight Deal. The Twilight Deal allowed admission to Kings Island for $15 per person after 4pm instead of the regular $45 per person. At the reduced price, our entire family was able to go and have a fabulous time! It is amazing how resourceful one becomes when required. I savored that trip to Kings Island more than any other due to my appreciation for our ability to save money *and* have fun.

My friend, Denise, invited me to a function titled, "The Fantasy Banquet" where the keynote speaker was Mrs. Mudd. She elaborated on how 'breakthroughs' result from assisting others which in turn helps one's self.

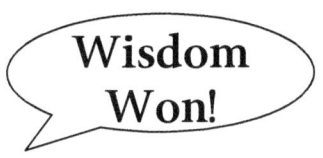

It is important to remain involved in activities to keep your mind stimulated. One method of staying engaged is to learn a new concept which can also provide a healthy mental escape.

For me, that took the form of Salsa dancing. While I enjoy dancing, I am not necessarily the best dancer. However, dancing and feeling the beat of the music starts my body swaying. In addition, the price to participate was perfect . . . free! I enjoyed myself immensely on account of opening myself to a new experience. Consider trying something different to broaden your horizons, to encounter different experiences as well as lift your mood.

Resist the urge to allow one aspect of your life to overshadow as well as dictate your outlook. Acknowledge the favorable things occurring in your life even in the midst of your situation.

I had concerns regarding how we would maintain our household on one salary and how long our savings would last. However, I gradually focused on what was going on outside of me and sought to help others. I have discovered fulfillment results from assisting others with a genuine motivation of making their life better.

Be resourceful by seeking out available discounts. It is amazing how you can think you are being a good steward of your money only to find out just how frugal you can become when necessary.

Before my job transition, I would have paid full price for a trip to an amusement park justifying my spending by saying it was not something we indulged in often. If I randomly located a $10 off coupon, it would have been just an added bonus not a necessity. However, in my new mindset I scoured the internet seeking to maximize our savings. Seek out reductions or other creative means to move forward with an event instead of canceling it altogether. Once you learn valuable information, share the knowledge with others to help them as well.

Idea

One day while I was eating lunch, I began to journal how I should write a book about lessons learned during my phase of unemployment. I thought about how I should have documented my entire experience of unemployment in greater detail. Once I reviewed my earlier entries I realized that I had captured more than I originally thought. This particular day marked the 125th day of my being unemployed. As I contemplated the prior 125 days, I recounted all I had accomplished during my time off that I could not have done had I been working.

I reconnected with my 92 year old great, great Aunt Lady taking her on errands as well as having her over for dinner during the week. I was able to rest and assess my next steps. A good friend shared with me that I was on her heart during her quiet time. She told me the word "rest" came to her mind when thinking of me as if this was a time of reprieve for me if I chose to view my situation in that manner.

Being available during the day afforded me the opportunity to work on a political campaign.

Regardless of one's political convictions, the entire 2009 Presidential campaign was historic. I canvassed neighborhoods meeting an array of people as I contributed service to my community. I voted early and volunteered at campaign headquarters which sparked a renewed interest in community service.

During my transition, I became an Environmental Awareness Board member. I have always had an interest in volunteerism and contributing to my community. Prior to having children, I was more involved but I have a renewed interest in volunteerism. While perusing my local newspaper I identified openings for several boards and commissions. I felt a pull to apply for the Environmental Awareness Board due to my desire to preserve and replenish our environment. I attended a meeting and knew immediately that it was the right choice. It was a dedicated group that was passionate about its purpose and mission. This allowed me to pay my gratitude forward while modeling community service for my children.

I planned a trip to South Beach, Florida for my husband's birthday in advance of my position being eliminated. Our vacation was paid in full therefore we continued with our plans. If you already had something planned prior to your change in circumstance and it is still feasible . . . proceed. Do not let uncertainty or worry prevent you. If circumstances make it such that it's not reasonable to progress with your plans, do not fret; another opportunity will surface.

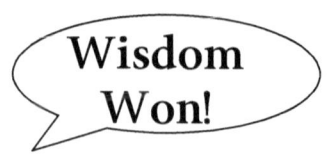

Experiences result in knowledge being acquired that, in turn, can be dispersed so that the wisdom obtained can be shared with others to aid them on their quest.

I had constant reminders that my job transition and all of its ramifications improved me in unimaginable ways. Concentrate on how a transition in your life can alter you for the better. The transformation may appear in the form of intangibles that could be easily overlooked if you're not careful such as building character, empathy for others and a stronger spiritual foundation.

Volunteerism is extremely rewarding. While contributing to the world at large you interact with interesting people; some not so unlike yourself thereby providing a broader perspective.

I have always felt *paying it forward* was a vital component to being involved in my community. However, my behaviors did not always reflect that mindset. I desired for my actions to support my beliefs along with providing an example of volunteerism for my children.

Move forward with any original plans if feasible. Let the creative juices flow to determine how you can make a planned activity happen instead of foregoing established plans.

Going ahead with our planned trip allowed us to take advantage of a change in scenery which was extremely beneficial. I have found that a mental escape is healthy while a physical escape is rejuvenating as well. Even if your diversion is to a local park or a stroll down your own street, you will be amazed at how your own surroundings can be relaxing, enjoyable, and possibly motivating.

Provided

My husband and I began a tradition early in our marriage of celebrating our birthdays by engaging in a unique activity or traveling somewhere new. In the past, we have been on a hot air balloon ride, gone rock climbing, scuba diving as well as many other adventures. This particular year, I thought it would be neat to mix it up and travel to a new destination for us, South Beach, Florida.

I made our vacation plans months in advance. I even secretly contacted my husband's boss to arrange his time off without him knowing it. My job was eliminated on July 15, 2008 with our trip planned for August 13, 2008. Many questions were swirling through my head. Do we still go? What makes sense? What's the right thing to do? After contemplating the situation, I felt the answer was to move forward since the trip was already paid in full. So we proceeded with our original plans still uncertain whether this was the best course of action.

The day prior to leaving, I learned the amount I would receive in unemployment benefits. The weekly amount was a drastic reduction to what I had contributed to our family's finances. While my husband and I discussed our funds he stated we needed to make some decisions. There was a heavy mood in our home, not the atmosphere you envision prior to vacation. I honestly was unsure of our next steps, but told my husband I felt that God wanted us to remember that He is still in control. He agreed and returned to his project.

I prayed about the heaviness that permeated our home requesting that God lift our burdens while helping us to trust Him. My children and I prepared to visit Meijer's to purchase groceries. I backed my car out of our driveway stopping at the mailbox to retrieve our mail. I placed the envelopes on the passenger seat while continuing my drive to Meijer's. I had been reading the Old Testament in detail seeking the passages of scripture where God was speaking. I desired to identify what He said, how He said it, and what the circumstances were so that I could discern God's direction for my life.

I stopped at the red light in front of Meijer's and began talking to God about how He is the God of Abraham, Isaac, and Jacob and how He provided for them. I reminded God that I am their descendant; therefore, the blessings they received applied to my family as well. Almost immediately after talking with God, I reached over and opened one of the envelopes from our mail revealing a check for $3,000! Tears streamed down my face as I attempted to maintain my composure while locating a parking spot. I called Donte' and told him through tears, that I was crying tears of joy! I shared with him that we received a $3,000 check that would pay all of our expenses thereby really allowing us to enjoy our trip. We hung up with each other and I continued to praise God for His goodness. My children were asking, "Mommy what's going on?" I shared the entire scenario because I wanted them to have a strong understanding, early in their lives, of God's goodness and how He provides in extraordinary ways.

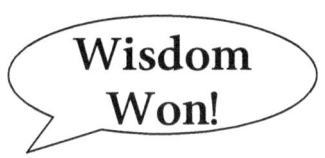

Wisdom Won!

It has been said, "you can't have a testimony without a test". A test in life is similar to an exam in school because it gauges strength in a particular area highlighting needed improvement. Having my prayer answered, regarding our finances, empowered my faith allowing me to continue on in the face of uncertainty.

There are striking similarities between educational and life tests. I was able to identify growth within myself as reflected by the peace I possessed. Even though I did not know my next step, I was not paralyzed by fear. I took each day one moment at a time.

Prayer definitely changes things; many times the person praying is also transformed. I have found that the answer may not be to eliminate a given situation I am in but to be given the grace and strength to navigate the circumstance successfully.
My prayer changed from, "Lord provide me with a job" to "help me identify my next opportunity". My ultimate desire became to glorify God knowing he always has my best interest at heart.

Do not limit how God can work in your life. When you see Him at work, acknowledge Him, thank him and give Him all the glory.
Some individuals might attempt to diminish God at work. In my specific circumstance it could be said that I would have received the $3,000 whether I

prayed or not. Perhaps, but I strongly believe things happen for a reason and at the correct time.

Flat

One day while driving on interstate 275 West I observed a piece of wood in my lane. In a split second I made sure there were no cars near mine that could be impacted by me braking and swerving to miss the obstacle. As I quickly changed lanes, my front driver's side tire ran over the edge of the board. While attempting to identify what I hit in my rearview mirror, I was hoping there was no nail in the board. I arrived home and did not give the incident another thought.

The next afternoon I was driving on Interstate 275 East on my way to pick up our children from school. As I drove over the seams in the road it seemed to me that I was hitting them extremely hard. However, it was cold outside so I thought maybe my tires were cold not giving it much thought. When I stepped out of my car to help my children get in and buckled up, one of the teacher's asked why I was not wearing a coat. I told her I went from our home to my car through the garage so I did not spend any significant time in the elements. I planned on going straight home so I would be fine.

Due to construction, what was normally a two lane ramp was temporarily narrowed to a single lane. I entered the ramp from Interstate 75 North towards Interstate 275 West. I heard a weird womp, womp, womp sound which I realized was the sound of my tire going flat. I quickly focused on maneuvering my car out of that single lane ramp over to the median for safety and so that we would not block traffic for hundreds of people. I desperately aimed for the median; however, it seemed like an eternity until we reached it. The median was reconfigured because of the construction so it was extremely narrow and close to the highway. I exited my car and saw that the front driver's side tire was flat as a pancake!

I usually have my cell phone with me; however, there have been times when I didn't because I'd forgotten it and didn't want to turn around in anticipation of being gone a brief time. I was extremely grateful that I did have my phone on that particular day. I found out earlier in the day that I used 289 minutes out of my 300 scaled back cell phone minutes. I decided I would turn my phone off and not use it until I had more minutes available. As I quickly thought all of this through, it came to mind to contact Verizon to determine what options were available to me. The Verizon representative informed me that because I called before I exceeded my established minutes, I was eligible for 50 additional minutes without charge! Praise God that's exactly what I needed! I told her thank you, contacted Geico to setup roadside assistance and called my husband. All of the necessary calls were made so then it was time to wait.

Cars, sports utility vehicles, and semi-trucks whizzed by us shaking our car. Snow flurries began to fall; however, I felt at peace. A Good Samaritan stopped, but I told him thank you; assistance was on the way. My children were asleep in the back seat so I took the opportunity to finish reading a book titled, "A Woman's Worth" that my stylist Bridgette let me borrow. There are positives to be found in every situation. I was thankful I did not lose control of my car, my children were asleep and warm, my car did not block the one lane ramp, and that it was still daylight. This experience reinforced the notion that one must always be prepared. I expressed to my children that mommy should have put a coat on instead of assuming I would return home directly. No one knows what can happen unexpectedly.

My husband, Donte', arrived at my car and then shortly thereafter the roadside assistance appeared. I prayed for the tow man's safety because he was only inches away from the highway but in no time he placed my spare tire on my car. Donte' suggested we obtain price estimates for a new tire right away; I agreed. We drove to a tire shop near our home. Keep in mind I am still without a coat feeling every bit of the cold at this point. I located a wool scarf in my trunk that I wrapped around my neck for some warmth. Once inside the tire shop our children indicated they needed to use the restroom. It dawned on me how fortunate I was that they did not have to use the facilities earlier!

The tire salesman provided us with an estimate that was more expensive than I anticipated. I thanked him stating that I wanted to obtain additional estimates. The estimate I received for the cost of the tire would have been a lot for me when I was working but now that I was unemployed – WOW! It was more than a notion! The thought came to mind that we *did* have the money available to pay for the tire. I did not have intentions to spend our money on a tire but fortunately the funds were there. I've heard people say they want to be blessed. What I am learning is that with bigger blessings come bigger responsibilities and costs. Although my car was a blessing to me, additional costs came with it.

    My appointment for having my new tire mounted was on a Sunday morning. Although I did not want to miss church I could no longer drive on my spare tire. While in the waiting room, I began to capture this entire flat tire episode in my journal. Interestingly enough, there was a spiritual television program playing on the television. I was glad to see the sales manager did not change the channel. I thought even though I did not physically attend church that morning my spirit was fed in the most unlikely place. Glory to God!

Prepare for the unexpected. Some events in life fall into the category of "when" not "if".
Leaving home without my coat was not a smart move. Being without a coat could be symbolic of how we enter certain situations in life. Are we leaving ourselves vulnerable and exposed to the elements by not having comprehensive wills, substantial savings, or the appropriate level of insurance? Typically it is prudent to a have a plan B in place for unexpected occurrences. However, a plan C may be in order as well when life takes a detour that is outside of your influence. I believe God is in control; but we have to execute our part. We have to participate in being good stewards.

Take unforeseen circumstances in stride. Events are not always as they appear on the surface. Maintain a positive attitude and continue to think clearly to navigate the situation at hand.
I am in no way stating I was happy I had a flat tire; however, I am learning that events are not always as they seem. Even though having that flat tire was inconvenient, the delay that it caused could have prevented me from being in a different place on the interstate where I could have been involved in a serious accident and harmed. We will probably never know some of the dangers we were protected from by some of the daily "inconveniences" we experience.

"Are you ready to be blessed?" is a saying I've heard over the years. I now have a better understanding regarding what this question means. Many times people say that they want a bigger home, a nicer car, etc., etc. . .

However, bigger and better comes with additional responsibilities and costs. It is important to make sure you are truly ready for what you are asking for and can handle the seen and unseen requirements that go along with that item.

Perspective

During December, 2008, I began reactivating my involvement in professional organizations such as Toastmasters and the Association of Certified Fraud Examiners (ACFE). My previous Toastmaster Club affiliations were through my employers where only employees were allowed to be members. Therefore, I located a Toastmasters club that was open to the public near my home. I attended a meeting and immediately felt that it was an active and progressive club. Reconnecting with Toastmasters provided a tremendous boost to my confidence while assisting me in maintaining my speaking skills as well as gaining new techniques to enhance my verbal communication. I located the local chapter of ACFE, and attended the member meeting with the intention of becoming an active member in the chapter.

I had obtained a fresh perspective and proceeded to accomplish a number of my goals. I secured a domain name and generated a website for my firm, Activate Consulting. I created a curriculum vitae when I applied for an adjunct faculty position.

It was an empowering exercise to compile all of my involvements and accomplishments throughout my career. This process reminded me I achieved a great deal in my past; therefore, I have the capability to do more of the same in my future. There is definitely a choice of how one views their circumstances. The perspective one holds will directly impact how one feels and the progress that is achieved.

As part of my quest to obtain some fresh perspective, I participated in Franklin Jentzen's 21-day corporate fast conducted at the beginning of each New Year. Fasting with a focus on God helped me simplify my life. It gave my body a rest from digesting solid food while providing me with much needed clarity. As a Christian, I view fasting as part of my walk according to Matthew 6:16-18; where fasting is spoken of in terms of "when you fast" and not "if you fast." I maintained a journal throughout my 21 days of fasting and began each day with meditation and prayer. I felt connected to my life in a much stronger way feeling strengthened spirituality, mentality and emotionally.

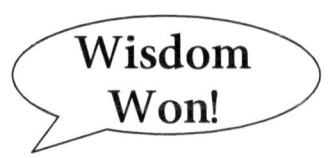

Continue or begin activities that you enjoy thereby helping yourself to develop as a person.
I found that my involvements made me accountable not only to myself but my fellow members. Exposure to other people with like interests is a fantastic means of learning to enhance your skill sets.

Put some action behind your dreams. Instead of talking about what you desire to accomplish, actually do it.
I have always wanted to operate my own company, so the next logical step for me was to create a website where prospective clients could receive more information. Think big; do not limit yourself to what you have achieved in your past. Stretch yourself; discover how to do something new.

Find what method is appropriate for you to feed your spirit and your mind as well as emotional well being.
Consider incorporating relaxation techniques into your routine. An activity as simple as taking deep cleansing breaths can be extremely effective in reducing stress while producing clear thoughts. Utilize visualization to envision yourself achieving a specific goal you have set. Writing your goals down makes them more tangible.

Appreciation

I cherish every blessing whether big or small, not taking them for granted. On my way to run errands I encountered two near miss car accidents. Thank you God for protection! Not only am I grateful for protection but also for restoration which results in my not having to spend money to replace an item I thought was lost. While shopping, I felt my earring fall out. I picked the earring up that I had just dropped putting it in my purse. I immediately checked my other ear and that earring was gone. I thought I would not be able to locate my other earring, because I had covered a lot of ground. However, when I arrived home I removed my scarf and out fell my missing earring. Praise God for that favor!

Saving money is a top priority for me. So imagine my dismay when our kitchen faucet broke. I searched Home Depot's shelves for a replacement kitchen faucet. While checking out the different price points, a lifetime warranty sign captured my attention. I became engrossed in the thought that the faucet I was looking to replace could possibly be fixed if it was under a lifetime warranty. I inquired of a salesperson whether the Moen brand faucet I desired to replace had a lifetime warranty as well. His response was music to my ears; yes the lifetime warranty applied to my faucet. The sales assistant was extremely helpful exhibiting wonderful customer service; God gave me favor with him. The sales person located the part that was needed to repair my faucet.

I drove home to obtain the faucet handle that broke off to ensure the correct placement parts were ordered. I hoped I could locate the faucet handle because I threw it away when it snapped off. I was grateful our trash collection day had not rolled around yet. I opened up the trash and found the faucet! I traveled back to Home Depot, found the associate so that he could identify the exact part. He first attempted to give me the replacement part from a new Moen faucet set off the shelf; however, it did not fit. He then contacted Moen on the phone, ordered the part at no charge to me and arranged for it to be sent directly to my home. The least expensive faucets I priced were around $129. Since exploring the limited warranty option, I've gone from paying a minimum of $129 to paying $0. Thank God for giving me favor and rebuking the devourer for our sake! Although our family did not have as much money entering our household, there was not as much going out. What a blessing! I delight in good, fortune no matter how minute or massive.

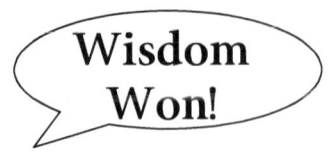

Take stock of the simple things in life that work in your favor. Depending on your situation, it may take some reflection to discover the good; but it is there.

Once you start focusing on positive aspects of your life, you will begin to attract favorable results in unexpected ways.

Identify opportunities to repair items instead of replacing them where possible.

I refurbished a pair of bar stools by spray painting them and recovering the seats with quality remnants from the fabric store. They actually look better than the originals now; if I do say so myself!

Usually how much one earns is not as important as how the money is managed.

Working in the financial services industry, I witnessed examples of high income clients that were not as savvy about managing their money as some lower income clients. When you are able to reduce your expenses, it has the same effect as increasing your income.

Pride

I was leaving Bed, Bath and Beyond when several women in the next car complimented my car stating that it looked nice. I replied by saying thank you describing it as a blessing. My children and I got into my car preparing to leave. In that moment, I became prideful thinking that I wanted them to see my personalized license plate. In hindsight, that thought does not even make any sense! I backed my car out of the parking space not remembering that I was next to a curb. I did not have enough clearance which resulted in me driving up over the curb with my front left tire. My tire came down from the curb with a loud *bam*! I got the attention I was looking for alright albeit not in the manner I envisioned! Everyone turned around to determine what happened; I was so embarrassed. My thoughts swirled – are we okay? Is there damage to my car? Why did this happen? The day had been so smooth with my faucet financial blessing at Home Depot and Christian, my son, finding $20. I felt God speak to my heart in that instant informing me that I went up on the curb because I let pride into my heart. I repented immediately. I told God, thank you for showing me myself reminding me of the need to remain humble. I learned my lesson praising God that my children were fine and there was no damage to be repaired. I took my eye off the ball and got smacked in the face. Pride tried to rear its ugly head again later that evening, but I saw it for what it was and repented. For a split second, I allowed myself to feel as though I was better than someone else. Lord, thank you for continuing to show me in what areas I need to improve.

The biggest room is room for improvement. Identify your strengths and weaknesses to work on enhancing your strong areas while correcting your areas of opportunity.
Being honest with myself regarding my behavior allowed me to assess where modifications were necessary. Maintaining integrity and honesty within oneself will begin to permeate other relationships resulting in a reputation of credibility.

Pride cometh before a fall. . .in some cases, this is a literal occurrence while in other instances it is more figurative.
In my case, I literally fell off the curb. However, if pride goes unchecked it can render relationships, jobs, and other areas of your life ineffective. Remain humble realizing it is God's grace that made your success achievable.

Heed the warnings in your life. I believe some events occur as a red flag to grab our attention.
I could have dismissed the incident with my car then maybe something of a greater magnitude would have happened to gain my attention. I am consciously aware of everyday occurrences. I no longer take situations for granted choosing to alter my mindset as circumstances dictate.

Hair

I began my hair journey in June, 2008, when I received my last permanent relaxer or perm for short. For more than 30 years I have had my hair relaxed resulting in my natural curl pattern being straightened. At this point in my life, I desired to stop the practice of having my hair permed. I was interested in seeing my natural hair texture. As I proceeded through this change, my hair routine involved washing my hair in the shower, wrapping it around my head while I slept, followed up by using a flat iron in the morning.

Flat ironing my hair worked extremely well to keep my hair looking nice even with my perm growing out. However, over a period of time my hair texture was too thick for my straightening routine. At that point, I began braiding my hair each night releasing the braids every morning. My nightly braiding resulted in a wavy bob hairstyle. While my perm continued to grow out exposing my natural texture at the roots, I began to notice curls along my neckline. I was excited to discover my natural texture; however, I was uncertain whether my hair would have the same texture throughout. At this phase in my hair journey, my hair was wavy near my scalp but straight on the ends resulting in it taking a lot of time to style.

On April 22, 2009 after almost a year of letting my perm grow out, I decided to cut out the remaining perm. I am so glad I cut my hair to reveal my natural texture. I have always liked what is called a *straw set* hairstyle which looks like small curls over the entire head. I never knew I naturally possessed that hairstyle all along! My hair transition has become such a metaphor for me that what I need or want in life in many instances is readily available for me to reveal. I took a risk cutting my hair without knowing how it would look. However, the risk was worth the reward due to achieving the style and freedom I desired. I style my hair in five minutes now when preparing my hair took so much longer in the past.

If you have always wanted to achieve a certain task begin fulfilling that desire; do not wait. Time never stops, so whether you are achieving your goals or not time is passing. You might as well utilize the time you have to accomplish your goals.

I am more innovative and creative than I realized. One area where I explored being unique was with my hairstyles. For you, it may be returning to school, traveling to new destinations, or approaching a special someone. Begin taking the steps to make your dream a reality.

Take calculated risks in life. Risks should be well thought out with a meaningful reward to be gained for taking the risks.

Throughout my 15+ years as a Risk Manager, I've learned there is no gain without taking risks. Be smart about the ventures in which you engage. Your level of exposure should be calculated and yield a comparable reward. To advance in your life pursuits, you must assume some level of risk.

Unveil the real you. Do you perceive that the life you are living does not align with your true essence?

For years, I felt as if I were a caged bird. I was successful at achieving what I was capable of doing but not what I was passionate about doing. I executed with excellence; however, I remained unfulfilled. Is the real you behind a facade or are you being your authentic self? If your answer is no, commit to making some changes.

Kindred

While meeting with Carson, Regional Dean for the Cincinnati location of a well respected university, he mentioned that I reminded him of another adjunct faculty member. Her name was Shelley and he described her as a very sharp person who was doing well in her role. I made a note of his statement for future follow-up to determine whether she was available to be my mentor. When my orientation was completed, I was informed that being assigned a mentor was the next step. I proactively inquired whether Shelley was available expressing how the Dean thought we might make a good partnership. Shelley and I were paired as mentor and mentee and I quickly felt a kindred connection. I take friendship seriously so imagine my amazement when within a short amount of time I considered Shelley a genuine friend. I admired her generosity with the knowledge she has attained as well as how honest she is with me regarding my performance and what I should implement to improve. I appreciate her mentorship and guidance more than she will ever know. I look forward to my opportunity to provide someone with insightful feedback in the manner that she has shared with me.

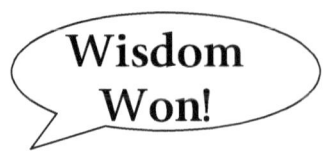

Wisdom Won!

While engaging in conversation, listen intently so that you can maximize beneficial information you receive.
While Carson was talking I might have missed the bonus information he stated if I were not listening intently. However, I paid close attention recognizing the importance of what was being stated. I'm a strong believer in taking notes to document critical details. Strong listening skills are essential. Two individuals can be privy to the same discussion with each person focusing on different aspects. If you can hone the skill of gleaning what is important, then act on that communication, you will benefit in unimaginable ways.

Be proactive in requesting what you want; don't hesitate to offer your insight. Frequently, people have not because they ask not.
I did not know if Shelley was available or willing to be my mentor but I inquired regardless. This is the case many times in life; we won't know what people are available or willing to do unless we ask. Don't essentially tell yourself no by not inquiring.

Interact with people in a genuine manner. One never knows when an acquaintance might develop into a valuable resource and good friend.
During my initial meeting with Shelley I was focused on learning from her by paying close attention to her experiences. She had been where I was attempting to

venture and had great wisdom to share. Being willing to learn from others allows you to gain different perspectives as well as make efficient use of your time by not recreating the wheel unnecessarily.

Preparation

My husband and I were fortunate that when we entered this transition of unemployment we did not possess credit card debt. However, we did hold a mortgage, a student loan, tuition payments, as well as two car notes. My previous car was 12 years old and paid off. I found it ironic that while I was employed I did not have a car payment and within a month of acquiring a car payment I became unemployed. I believe that God knowing my vehicle would soon be defunct set a plan in motion for me to obtain a new car. Without prodding, I would not have purchased a new car. My motto was, "I am going to drive my car until it stops on the side of the road". Not only did it stop on the side of the road, but the repairs were so extensive that it was not cost effective to repair it. Instead I donated it to a local charity.

Since God knew what was about to transpire in my life, I believe he placed me in a position to obtain another car. He knew about my pending unemployment and understood I needed a reliable vehicle instead of one requiring countless repairs. If my car could be restored for a reasonable price, I would have continued to fix it which was not the best investment. My husband and I negotiated a great deal at the end of the month on a pre-owned car. We made a sizeable down payment to reduce the monthly payment to a reasonable amount.

Since my car purchase occurred a month before my job was eliminated, admittedly my first reaction was, "God, why did you allow me to acquire this car knowing that my job would be eliminated?" I felt Him respond that He desired to bless me. The timing was right in terms of the car being available and us locating the vehicle. He assured me that my job elimination did not nullify that timing. If my car would have broken down after my job elimination, it would have been difficult to purchase a vehicle in spite of our excellent credit rating due to no longer having a salary in a weakened economy. God demonstrated how His timing works for my good even when his methods appear unconventional. I am discovering the importance of preparation for the unexpected. I believed I was diligent in handling our money; however, it became clear that I could regulate our funds more efficiently. My ultimate goal is to owe no man anything but to love him with all of our financial obligations paid in full.

Be prepared for the unexpected. Many people have not properly prepared for a job elimination or an extended period of unemployment, myself included.

We maintained a decent amount of savings; however, we were not as strategic when it came to earmarking the recommended emergency fund. As I have learned through experience, as have so many others, it is crucial to retain an emergency fund as prescribed by financial experts.

The manner in which situations unfold might not make sense in the present; however, it will become clearer in the long term.

I viewed my situation through a "right now" filter; however, I believe God was looking at what would benefit me in the future. Whether or not *we* think we can handle a given situation God knows how much we can bear.

Being financially sound is vital to one's well being. Financial security does not necessarily mean having large sums of money but properly managing the money that is at your disposal.

It is prudent to have more financial resources coming into your household than are being disbursed, to keep your finances along with other areas of your life in balance and harmony.

Receiving

When I requested financial aid from my children's school we were awarded a reduction in tuition; however, we did not qualify for full assistance. The financial aid process is based on prior year tax returns instead of immediate need. I believe a provision should be included in the financial aid approval process that provides a better measure of a person's current financial status. The prior year tax returns I submitted reflected my previous salary in addition to my husband's salary. The information contained in that tax return was meaningless as soon as my financial contributions were eliminated. My salary a year ago became irrelevant since my current contribution was minimal. Although, my income level decreased drastically we still had the same amount of expenses.

I decided that when I was in a position to do so, I would establish a fund for individuals who appear to be thriving on paper but hit a bump in the road. I became aware of a gap in terms of help for individuals in a middle income bracket that need to maintain a level of savings while adjusting to sudden financial changes.

I think the art of giving is discussed and practiced more than the art of receiving, not "taking" but *receiving*. I know there are individuals that have difficulty with giving, but it seems to me that many people enjoy giving. At times, the same people that enjoy giving find it difficult to receive, particularly those who are self-sufficient. Admitting that one needs help or being willing to receive assistance can be hard. I have discovered that one must have the capacity to receive to be capable of giving.

I mentioned to my husband how it had been a while since I went to the salon and how it would be great to have my hair professionally styled. No sooner than I shared my desire with him I received a text message from my stylist inviting me to a courtesy hair service at a time that worked for my schedule. I could not believe that her offer was right in line with what I had been thinking. She even proposed my coming on a day that she normally does not work if that would be more convenient.

As soon as I received the text from her, I decided that I would still pay her although she stated there was no cost. I reasoned within myself, if nothing else, that I would provide a generous tip. Once I arrived at Bridgette's salon, she explained the story behind the text message she sent. She shared how I had been on her mind prompting her to draft a text message inviting me to come for a complimentary hairdo. Knowing that I was seeking a new opportunity she wanted me to be confident about my hair. She revealed when she began typing the text it was late so she planned to send the message the next day. Two days later, as she prepared to send a text to someone else she saw the unsent text she had prepared for me. When she discovered the unsent text message, she sent it immediately.

I saw this as divine intervention, God's timing is awesome! If Bridgette had sent the text when she originally compiled it, that would have been fine; however, I believe God used this situation to remind me he is in control still working on my behalf even when I do not realize it! This demonstrated how people are thinking about you even when you don't know it. When I arrived at Bridgette's salon, I planned to compensate her in spite of her generous offer. Prepared for how I would try to circumvent her offer, since she knew me so well, she had planned ahead for my protest. Overwhelmed by her generosity tears began to stream down my face. In that moment, I decided to avail myself to receive as well as enjoy my complimentary hair service!

It can be difficult to understand the plight others are experiencing until that condition becomes personal. Many times situations occur to heighten our awareness to the adversity of others.
I cultivated deeper empathy for people in need of an interim solution, particularly when I became one of them. I am more acutely aware of the needs of others assessing how I can support their efforts. Be sensitive to what is important to others, then determine how you can assist.

Being unwilling to receive prevents the person attempting to contribute from receiving the joy of giving along with possibly blocking their blessing.
Instead of my normal, "No, you don't have to do that." I now say, "thank you" accepting with gratitude the kindness being shown. People realize they are not obligated to extend a kindness to you so when they offer, they genuinely want to help or bless you.

People who are accustomed to giving may find it difficult to find themselves on the receiving end.
Similar to a pitcher of water being poured into drinking glasses, once it has been emptied out it has to be refilled from the water source to continue pouring into other receptacles. As people, it is a good thing to give by pouring into other's lives, but we must remember to replenish ourselves from our source, which, at times, is directly from God in the

form of much needed rest and relaxation or from a dear friend being sensitive to your need.

Rebranding

Recruiters are one avenue to utilize when seeking your next opportunity; however, they should not be the only method of marketing yourself to companies. I found I had to take steps to rebrand myself. My previous job title of Internal Audit Director caused some recruiters as well as organizations to have a limited perception of my accomplishments in that role.

My 15 plus years of work experience was mainly concentrated in the Internal Audit field. At times, the depth and breadth of my role as an internal auditor was not as clearly understood as the role of an external auditor. While there are broad similarities between internal and external auditors some differences are also present. Frequently, an internal auditor's scope of coverage is broader regarding the nature, extent and timing of testing than what was required of an external auditor. This is due, in large part, to the internal auditor being able to focus on one specific company. Materiality levels are usually higher for external auditors for them to attest on certain account groups in an efficient manner so that they can move on to their next audit client. While internal auditors also work with efficiency and effectiveness, they have more of an opportunity to conduct more detailed testing than their external counterparts.

While two main objectives for all auditors are to attest to the soundness of the financial statements and the viability of the company being audited, there are opportunities for internal auditors to perform duties that extend beyond pure financial work. As an internal auditor, along with executing financial and operational audits, I also established entity-wide risk management frameworks, and worked with management to strengthen internal controls, monitoring, and oversight. I provided guidance and direction on fraud prevention and fraud detection techniques as well as conducted internal control training for corporate and field personnel among many other tasks.

It became evident after speaking with a number of recruiters that they were limiting my job search to traditional accounting and auditing roles without taking into consideration my broad and non-traditional skill sets. I was placed in a specific category based on my position title without being assessed based on my various skill sets to identify different opportunities for which I was qualified. This obvious need to rebrand my experience and professional background led me to rework my resume. Instead of highlighting my specialized internal audit role, I focused on my broader role as a Risk Management Professional. I conveyed how I utilized auditing to gain an understanding of internal controls and risk environments. This brought more attention to the depth and breadth of my experience.

Do not narrowly define your talents, skill sets, and abilities solely by a prior job title. I have discovered that job titles can be limiting with the meaning varying greatly depending on the company.

When I stopped and took an inventory of my skill sets, they were many and varied. I edited, trained, facilitated, coached, empowered, directed, created, wrote and the list continues. I may not have received formal training in each of these areas; however, performing them for so long throughout my career I became proficient in them. Consider highlighting the broader aspects of your skill sets providing relevant examples to support your competency.

Some recruiters that I had the pleasure of working with were superb while others were not attentive or thorough. I quickly learned that I needed to function as my own best advocate.

I am a proponent of one being responsible for one's career success. I had to remind myself that being accountable for my own career did not change with me becoming unemployed. I made certain when working with recruiters that I was explicit with how I wanted to be represented as well as how my experiences and background should be conveyed to fully demonstrate my value.

Some attributes only emerge when more prominent characteristics are not in the forefront as much. I reached the current place in my life by allowing my less evident skill sets to manifest instead of relying solely on the talents I utilized most in the past.

Had my position not been eliminated, I might not have engaged in an in-depth assessment of what I have achieved in the past while contemplating all I have to offer. While focusing on the concealed parts of myself, I uncovered enriching aspects of my personality. Take time to reconnect with yourself, catalogue your numerous traits and maximize your abilities.

Networking

When my position was eliminated, my business cards were null and void since my prior employer's information was included. If outplacement services are offered to you, consider using the business card option along with other relevant offerings. Specifically, the business cards proved to be beneficial for networking. A person that is seeking their next opportunity may find it helpful to have business cards that include at a minimum their name, title as well as contact information. If you are not given the outplacement options, consider creating your own business cards using a service like VistaPrints.com. I found that VistaPrints.com provided quality products for a reasonable price.

Though I found myself "in between" positions, I discovered that I could still contribute to mutually beneficial networking relationships by sharing my contacts as well as utilizing my involvements on boards and service organizations. One can be lulled into equating their ability to network with being employed. When I was initially unemployed, I felt at a disadvantage when it came to networking due to not having the influence I once possessed at a particular company. I was quickly reminded that networking is not constrained by the walls of a company or my title but by the relationships I've established and maintained.

For example, maybe a person is volunteering their services during their unemployment. Although this person is not employed, they could be a restaurant guru knowing all of the best places to eat in the city. A reliable recommendation about a local restaurant can be immensely valuable for someone looking to entertain as well as impress a client. This is just one instance of how broad one's influence can be in spite of not being employed.

Some individuals think they do not have time to network; however, the opposite is true - you don't have time to *not* network. Yes, it takes time to build genuine relationships; however, those relationships are an investment that generates significant benefits over time. Networking should become a priority that is continually developed resulting in a mutual flow of reciprocal acts. I have found that a mutual exchange is truly the essence of networking.

As I discussed earlier in this book, an executive recruiter spoke briefly about the BNI networking organization. She mentioned it in passing, but I took note of what she stated in order to research it later. Maintaining sharp listening skills is critical because valuable information can be obtained even if it is ancillary to the conversation. I encourage you to enhance your listening skills to determine how you can assist someone else meet their need; this will pay dividends in goodwill.

Once I conducted some quick research, I discovered that BNI was one of the largest business networking organizations in the world! It is amazing how many resources are available if only we are made aware of them. Imagine how pleased I was when I was invited to attend a local BNI networking session. While there, I learned to consider everyone as a potential connection such as my real estate agent and hairstylist, to name a few. Sometimes as we begin building a support team as well as advocates for our next steps, we don't think to incorporate people we come in contact with regularly.

Participate in professional organizations, functioning in a leadership role where feasible. Exude confidence doing your best with whatever task to which you commit. Fellow members will then be able to endorse you based on your work ethic as well as other positive attributes even though they have not worked with you in a professional capacity. Familiarize yourself with a broad spectrum of individuals. More importantly, allow them to become acquainted with you, your character and abilities. Then when an opportunity arises, you will be the person that is considered.

Maintain contact with people in your network that is being established. Create reminders either in an Outlook calendar or database to capture relevant information gained from key conversations. Follow up periodically to maintain the connection as well as stay informed about their current needs. This will enable you to assist them in accomplishing their professional goals that might align with your own.

I attended a networking function where I sat next to a gentleman that on the surface may not have appeared to have anything in common with me. However, I did not allow that to prohibit me from striking up a conversation. I shared with him that I was an active Toastmasters member. He expressed an interest in learning more about this organization. At one point we exchanged business cards, I discreetly wrote on the back of his card the interest in Toastmasters. I told him I would provide detailed information for the next meeting. I contacted him by e-mail immediately after the event before my commitment was forgotten or too much time elapsed. I made a cyber introduction between him and my club president sharing the dates, times, and locations of our meetings. Our earlier conversation was still fresh in both of our minds solidifying the positive impression that was made in person.

Prompt follow up demonstrates that a person is reliable, values integrity, and keeps their word. These values have a lasting impact. Only extend yourself to others if you are truly committed to fulfill any stated obligations, because you can quickly gain a reputation for being unreliable if commitments are repeatedly abandoned. You want to be viewed as a "can do" person instead of someone who over commits and under delivers.

Be visible in your professional community by participating in your local chapters, being published in a business publication or volunteering to give a presentation about your professional subject matter. Your involvement will create a buzz possibly serving as a means to secure future business or a career opportunity you desire.

Prepare an engaging 30 second "commercial" about yourself including what you can offer so that you are prepared when someone expresses an interest in knowing more about you. In addition, be able to answer the following question, "What can I do for you?" if a person of influence should ask. People are willing to help you open doors as well as be your advocate once they become acquainted with your character and abilities. However this is contingent on being able to verbalize wants in a concise yet specific manner.

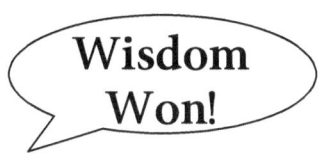

Do not diminish what you can contribute to a networking relationship.
Even as your circle of contacts expands to the point where it includes individuals that are already well connected, don't be intimidated. Listen to what they have going on in their lives paying attention for opportunities to assist them with their needs.

There is a difference between hearing someone speak versus truly listening to them. Strive to place an emphasis on listening.
Where appropriate, take notes to remind yourself about key points in a conversation. I usually have a journal with me to write down impromptu ideas and capture important information.

If someone walked up to you and asked you what you wanted to do and how they could help, would you be prepared to respond in a manner that is specific yet concise?
Prepare a 15-30 second infomercial about yourself. Imagine you are on an elevator with seconds to make a great first impression. What will you say to engage that person leaving them wanting to know more?

Words

Write your aspirations down, say them out loud, and then prepare for your assertions to come to fruition. Words are extremely powerful! I believe strongly that one manifests what they say, speaking out of what is believed in their heart. It has been said, it is better to be prepared and not have an opportunity than to have an opportunity present itself and not be prepared. I discovered that some things will only materialize for me when I do what I know I need to do today.

Moving forward without access to the entire picture can be daunting. I have learned that there are times when I must take one step before my next move will be revealed. I refuse to operate in fear opting to view uncertainty as an adventure. In many ways, I can create what I want to happen. I recall hearing a statement that I thought was extremely poignant - if you want to know the future, create it! Granted there are circumstances beyond our control; however, we can regulate our reaction to a given situation. When my job was eliminated I could have allowed myself to feel that I did not deserve that treatment posing the question "why me?" I knew that type of thinking was counterproductive for me, my family as well as my continued well-being. Definitely, experience the full bevy of emotions that are present; however, don't allow yourself to wallow or remain in that place too long. Continued despair is toxic to your future success.

Create what you desire in life with your words. I believe I was destined to write, among other things, using the written form of communication to positively impact society. Although my formal education was not focused on writing; that did not prevent me from working to hone this ability. Before I could expect anyone else to respect my writing skills, I had to take my own work seriously. The date I truly deemed myself a writer was February 11, 2009. I completed the required paperwork in preparation for a routine eye exam. In the occupation section of the form, I wrote consultant/author representing my consulting firm established in 2001 that was rebranded in 2009 as well as for writing the book you are reading now. My doctor entered the room and stated, "Oh you are an author." I replied, "I am in the process of writing a book." He responded, "that definitely makes you an author. When you sell many books, then you will be a *successful* author. But today, right now, you are an author." That reinforced my desire along with my mindset to regard myself as an author. Dr. Burns, my optometrist, probably had no idea the power his words contained. This exchange provides a great example of how we might never know the life changing properties our words hold.

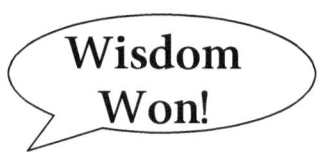

Declare positive affirmations throughout your day as well as carve out some quiet time to gain inspiration, cultivate ideas and obtain clarity.
If an idea or concept consistently stays on your mind, more than likely it is meant for you to act on it. Conduct research, weigh the pros as well as cons, then take a calculated risk that will yield comparable rewards. You might not see how your aspiration will unfold in its entirety; however, focus on achieving the portion of the overall plan that you are inspired to do.

Be proactive about pulling your dreams into reality. Imagine events in your life as though they have already occurred. View things that aren't as though they are then open your mouth announcing what you want to happen. Visualizing and proclaiming go hand in hand.
I considered myself an author well in advance of selling my first book. I determined in my heart that I possessed an untapped ability that I needed to liberate. Let's remind ourselves often that no one can accomplish what we were placed on this Earth to achieve. Write down specifically what you want to happen in your life within the next six months maintaining it in a place where you view it daily. Taking this proactive step will prompt you to put those words into action.

Words are extremely powerful being described as sharper than a two-edged sword. Words can build a person up or tear them down.

Contemplate the effect your words have on your spouse, children, friends as well as other people in your life. Most importantly how are your words, thoughts and outward declarations affecting you? Do you speak positive affirmations building yourself up or destroy yourself with negativity?

Inspiration

It is amazing how inspirations can come from seemingly unlikely sources. I was moved by the movie titled *The Women* released in 2008. Meg Ryan's character went through a difficult time in her life where her emotions ran the gamut leaving her in a rut. One of the tools she utilized as she emerged from her difficulties was a vision board. Prior to seeing that movie, I heard how an Olympian created a vision board depicting herself winning a gold medal then she achieved just that! Hearing about the Olympian's success in addition to seeing the vision board in *The Women* movie confirmed that I needed to create my own.

There is something about having goals depicted in pictures to reinforce the direction in which one is heading. An acquaintance shared with me how she wrote her goals for 2009 as if they were already fulfilled. Why not implement her technique of projecting specifically what you desire for your future? You have nothing to lose with everything to gain.

The Disney movie, *Meet the Robinsons*, was an encouragement to me as well. This movie demonstrates how the destiny of various individuals would have been altered if the main character quit when he did not initially succeed. The dynamics of this movie strengthened my resolve to continue striving to fulfill my purpose. Instead of giving up when things looked bleak, I kept plugging away giving my best effort.

Speaking of best, a scene in the film *Facing the Giants* provided a powerful visual of what "delivering your all" looks like. The specific scene depicts a young man extending beyond what he thought was possible. I questioned whether I truly stretched myself exhibiting excellence in absolutely everything I do. There were some areas where I definitely saw room for improvement. Certain areas I have been honing are my consistency, discipline and focus.

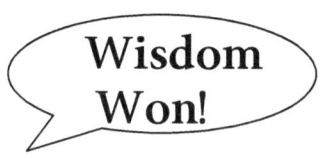

You can glean inspiration as well as insight from a variety of sources. Maintain an awareness of your surroundings to appreciate the deeper meaning in everyday occurrences.

As a result of my transition, I became more conscious of what is important to me being cognizant of my environment along with the individuals around me.

A vague understanding of where one pictures himself in the future leads to either not generating goals at all or being too general in what is trying to be achieved.

I did not know exactly how I would achieve the goals I had in mind, but I maintained a visual of my desired end result. For example, I could have hoped someone, by chance, would have called me to be an adjunct professor or I could have chosen to proactively fill out an application then follow up to express my sincere interest in the opportunity. I chose the latter.

Don't settle for less. When it comes to relationships, jobs or other areas of our lives we set a standard of expecting more. However, do we hold ourselves to that same level?

Expect the same intensity from yourself as you would anticipate from someone else. Continue to challenge yourself stretching beyond your prior personal best.

Reconnect

It is now approximately six months after my job elimination and I had contacted every lead I knew. My family and friends shared their contacts with me as well. However, no jobs materialized. I've been told that hiring slows during the holiday season; now I was experiencing that phenomenon personally. I resolved to begin my job search anew in January.

An acquaintance, who was a Human Resource professional in transition as well, scheduled a Wednesday networking meeting at Panera Bread. Her vision was to provide an informal gathering where people could share information, contacts, resume ideas, and job leads along with receiving encouragement. I was anticipating the first meeting in early January.

I realized while preparing for the initial network meeting that I had become isolated as well as a bit depressed. I stood in my closet thinking about how much time had elapsed since I had an occasion to put on a nice shirt, slacks or blazer. I was officially in a rut wearing mainly sweats and tshirts. Granted, there is nothing wrong with this attire especially since it is comfortable as well as low maintenance. However, I was approaching the point of letting myself go without even realizing it. I figured I was not going anywhere, so I did not need to dress as if I were. The problem arose because I was not heading anywhere physically or figuratively.

I was amazed at how rejuvenated I felt by putting on my own pressed clothes along with spending time on my hair and makeup. Looking pulled together on the outside really gave me a boost on the inside! When I arrived at the gathering, I knew immediately this was exactly what I needed. Being transparent, I shared with the group how getting dressed along with having somewhere to go did me a world of good.

Conversing with individuals who were in transition like me and who understood what I was dealing with was validating. We shared our professional backgrounds along with our passions and pursuits. Each member provided guidance to one another as well as accountability. At the end of the session, we ensured everyone had an assignment for the following week based on what they were looking to accomplish. I am grateful for people like Amelia who have an idea, then act on it. She will probably never know the positive impact she has had on my life, specifically the benefits I gained from her organizing our Wednesday morning gatherings at Panera.

The professionals that met on Wednesday mornings discussed how in Cincinnati, the 6 degrees of separation is more like 3 degrees, due to so many people knowing each other. To be successful in a job search as well as other areas of life, one has to gain exposure, be visible, along with building strong relationships. Julie, a member of the network group, was extremely generous with her contacts as well as her "can do" attitude. Instead of giving up in a difficult situation, she determined how she could make things happen. She was the inspiration I needed, because she shared candid situations of how she took calculated risks that worked to her advantage. Her philosophy was, if someone tells me "no", I am no worse off than I am currently. Her attitude on life exemplifies "how can I make this work?" instead of "I can't". I admire that about her.

Once again, my support system held me accountable giving me a needed push in the right direction. My fellow colleagues provided me with perspective on a goal for the number of clients I should contact each day. From Julie's pharmaceutical days, she stated her goal was to communicate with a minimum of 10 doctors daily. She indicated I could utilize a similar benchmark to gauge the number of contacts by e-mail, phone call, lunch, or handwritten note that I should strive to attain each day for potential clients. I implemented this level of contact immediately.

As a result of our meeting, I saw that I needed to enhance my networking. I thought I was an effective networker; however, I was striving to expand my contact base. I sat down to think about the professional organizations with which I was affiliated to begin renewing my memberships along with my commitment to participate in local chapter meetings. I've been an active member with Toastmasters for many years, but I let my involvement lapse as a result of my job transition. I located my Toastmaster binder that included all of my speeches to identify my next speech. I searched on the internet for a public Toastmaster club with a proximity to my home. I found a club that met every 1st and 3rd Thursday and placed the upcoming meeting on my calendar.

Being a Risk Management professional, I sought a local risk organization and found the Risk and Insurance Management Society, Inc. (RIMS). Their website contained the next meeting date which I made plans to attend. I also have my Certified Fraud Examiner certification, so I decided to participate in the next local Association of Certified Fraud Examiner's (ACFE) chapter meeting. Having those meetings scheduled on my calendar made me feel that I was moving in the right direction. I anticipated meeting new connections while expanding my horizons.

Soon thereafter I was notified that I was selected to be an Adjunct Faculty member at a well-respected university. Although, I would facilitate part-time, that was the boost I needed! Teaching is a pursuit I have envisioned myself performing, so to have my assignment be at a faith-based university was a bonus.

Throughout my period of transition, it was important for me to stay connected instead of allowing myself to become isolated. Individuals in my life assisted me with remaining involved more than they probably realized. I've gone from being secluded to encountering new people every day. I think time spent by yourself is beneficial as well as a component of one's overall journey. However, I don't believe you are meant to remain in a place of solitude for an extended period of time.

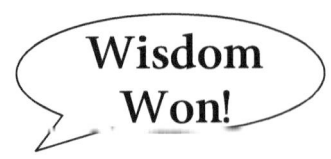

Maintain a routine providing structure to ensure that you make your mental as well as physical health a priority.
Preparing for the networking meeting was a reality check for me. Utilize my reality check to provoke yourself into action where needed in your life. Are areas of your well being neglected? If so, it is time to reclaim those aspects of your life.

Accountability is always important, but the need is heightened during a transition. Make yourself responsible to someone that you interact with regularly.
Share goals you desire to attain within a specified timeframe. At various intervals, provide a status on your progress. Knowing that you have to answer to an outside party regarding your achievement helps to maintain focus as well as motivation.

Sometimes the question we pose initially is, "where do I begin"? Maybe one perceives the need to take a different approach but what should be the first step?
The first step taken varies based on the individual situation. A good method to tackle this question is to include those who know you well that can relate to your circumstance. Identify a person of integrity to talk to that will provide constructive feedback or consider joining an appropriate organization for support.

Connections

I attended my first RIMS meeting at the Banker's Club on January 23. The first person I saw was a prior colleague I invited to attend the meeting. We chatted for a few moments then began to mingle with the rest of the group. As I introduced myself, I listened intently to people I met giving my full attention to what was being said. I thought I was a good listener before but I realized that I could enhance that skill. As I obtained business cards from people I met, I discreetly wrote a memorable fact to remind me of the person thereby facilitating my follow up.

For example, while speaking to one gentleman I mentioned that I was an adjunct faculty member at a well-respected university. He expressed an interest in knowing about my experience as an adjunct professor, because he considered pursuing that path in the future. I wrote on the back of his business card, "interested in adjunct experience" to facilitate future communications. Immediately following the event I sent e-mails to each person, from whom I obtained business cards, stating that I enjoyed meeting them along with inquiring whether they would be interested in a breakfast or lunch meeting to facilitate a better understanding of our respective projects.

When I e-mailed the gentlemen with the interest in becoming an adjunct faculty member, I told him I would keep him informed regarding teaching opportunities. I realized networking does not have to be forced. I had to initially pursue each connection, but a short while later some connections took on a life of their own. That is what happened with Andy, another person I met at the RIMS meeting. The topic of the RIMS meeting was networking which was very appropriate since due to my job elimination, I was laser focused on making mutually beneficial connections.

The keynote speaker represented the outsource company I used during my transition. Andy was seated at my table a few chairs down from me. All of the individuals at the table were engaged in great conversation. Andy mentioned how it was beneficial to be published in industry periodicals to gain visibility along with creating opportunities to meet as well as help new people. Andy stated that he sends relevant articles to contacts as well as prospective clients, writing his own article if he cannot locate a good one.

I e-mailed Andy telling him that it was a pleasure meeting him and asked would he be interested in a breakfast or lunch meeting to learn about our respective initiatives. Not only did he agree but he shared articles he had written. I e-mailed to confirm the date telling him I would read his articles then share my thoughts. I wanted to ensure I gave his articles my full attention. Andy's articles were fantastically original! I am a visual person who prefers practical information I can apply. His articles conveyed business principles in a unique; however, extremely effective manner. He utilized the example of how well salons create loyalty between stylist and client. He expressed how the listening skills of the stylist are essential in meeting the client's needs. Maintaining an attentive ear helps with setting subsequent appointments in advance which leads to increased repeat business, a solid customer base and higher profits. I spent time compiling my comments regarding his articles. Instead of providing generalized feedback I shared the specific points that appealed to me.

At a later date, we did have an opportunity to meet for lunch. Andy was personable, funny, as well as generous with helpful information. I admire these characteristics and desire to exude them when others interact with me. He told me he viewed my web site which I really appreciated! I delayed publishing my website to the internet due to it not being exactly as I desired. Julie, from my networking meeting, implored me to launch my web site and continue to refine it in phases. So for Andy to demonstrate an interest by taking time to review my web site as well as provide meaningful feedback made me feel validated for my efforts.

His behavior modeled for me the interest level I need to demonstrate when interacting with others. I felt extremely motivated as a result of having such a productive conversation. One never knows the encouragement a simple gesture may provide. I enjoyed our lunch on a number of levels. Our business discussion gave way to a more in-depth conversation about our individual personalities and backgrounds. Andy shared that he and his wife had been married 30 years. I took that revelation as an inspiration for my husband and I who had been married 12 years at that time. At the conclusion of our lunch, I had a wealth of ideas, mutual accountability about our next steps for our individual businesses, as well as a lifelong friend.

In the past, I obtained business cards then allowed valuable relationships to slip through my fingers due to a lack of follow-up that is needed to keep the connection current. I created a database of vital contacts that now prompts me to follow-up periodically. I maintain brief information reminding me what initiatives are important to each person, as well as identify opportunities to link like-minded individuals.

Andy challenged me on the following points during lunch: clear identification of my target market, establishing a call to action for my website along with a frequently asked question section to answer pertinent inquires. He recommended that when I made updates to my website that I send out an e-mail soliciting feedback to create a buzz possibly procuring new clients. He suggested including the link to my website to make people aware that I requested their feedback due to respecting their opinion.

As a result of our meeting, I knew I needed to create a client presentation describing my company philosophy along with services offered. Around the same time, I scheduled my 8th Toastmaster speech towards completing my Competent Communicator designation. I was inspired to prepare one presentation for both purposes. Amazingly, once I began the presentation it really flowed. I delivered the speech during my Toastmasters meeting where I received valuable feedback. In addition, I was awarded the best speaker award for my efforts. The opportunity to speak enables me to build confidence conveying my skills in a forum where I obtain honest unbiased feedback.

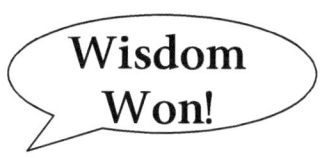

It is prudent to employ a method of recalling details about individuals you meet.
Business cards have proven to be a useful tool for me. I realize others may prefer entering contact information directly into their handhelds or other technological devices. Whatever your preference, ensure pertinent details are captured to lay the foundation for a genuine relationship.

Become accustomed to approaching individuals that, on the surface, appear unlike you. You might be surprised what you have in common as far as interests and aspirations.
Share appropriate personal disclosure about yourself. Mentioning my involvement with Toastmasters disclosed a common topic. Although you may not make a connection with everyone you meet, the bonds you do create will be more meaningful.

Learn from the positive examples of people who are generous with their resources as well as their insights. Use their behavior as a blueprint of how you should strive to treat others.
My faith in people was restored by the actions of a few individuals who demonstrated their willingness to help me succeed. Their behavior served as inspiration for me to mirror the same actions for others.

Feedback

Julie introduced me to two of her close friends, Molly and Arlene. I thanked her for the referrals then contacted both Molly and Arlene to determine whether they were available for a breakfast or lunch meeting. I desired to share my initiatives while understanding how I could assist them with their pursuits. Fortunately, both ladies were willing to meet with me. These professional women were experienced business owners so I was looking forward to gleaning from their practical knowledge. After exchanging a few e-mails, we settled on dates and times. Don't be discouraged if when you arrange meetings the date ends up being further in the future than you anticipated, due to busy schedules, because everything happens in its right timing.

I agree that the benefits of networking are tremendous; however, I saw that I could be more deliberate in my efforts. I have found when I focus on helping the other person in a networking relationship, the exchange was fluid not forced or contrived. As an example, prior to the date Molly and I agreed to meet, Julie sent me an e-mail detailing the need for volunteers to participate in a focus group for Molly's company. Being open to new experiences, I replied that I would participate. I was glad to support Molly's efforts providing a mutual benefit which is the essence of networking. The day Molly and I met in person was the Friday before her focus group session the following Monday.

I discovered that Molly and I possessed similar backgrounds. She also worked in the corporate world. Then as a result of her personal passion, she launched her own company which was one of my aspirations. Our meeting was informative. I appreciated the opportunity to interact with a strong woman who was actively fulfilling her dream. I respected her honesty in admitting that beginning her own venture was challenging but well worth it. She provided encouragement as well as practical feedback which I immediately implemented. She graciously agreed to meet periodically allowing me to share ideas with her as well as gain insights from a seasoned business owner. This is another relationship that I am determined to cultivate.

The focus group that I participated in for Molly was excellent! I felt honored to be involved, share my feedback, as well as be enriched by the experience. The concept she was launching was destined for success due to creating a needed paradigm shift. I struck up a conversation with Mary, the woman who sat next to me during the focus group session. We engaged in a discussion where we described our respective backgrounds. She mentioned that a good friend of hers, Terry, had a similar background as mine working for a local fraud firm. I told Mary I recently spoke to her friend on the phone to obtain information about the local ACFE chapter meetings. Mary offered to formally introduce me to her friend Terry. I told her I really appreciated the opportunity to become familiar with Terry prior to meeting her in person at the ACFE meeting. Mary invited me to join her LinkedIn page as well as her personal networking group. Her willingness to include me in her networks reaffirmed how important it is to avail myself to meet people, share, and listen as well as assist. The fact that so many people are intertwined means each connection could branch out to numerous alliances.

Take initiative to extend yourself to those with whom you have been put into contact. Even when you receive good information, it does not work effectively until acted upon.
Be timely in follow-up. This assists the other person in recalling who you are setting the expectation for future contact. I was linked with potential contacts that could have become stagnant had I not followed up with them in a timely manner.

New opportunities emerged because I was willing to first help someone else.
I agreed to join the focus group because I thought it would be interesting, as well as allow me to demonstrate my support. Expose yourself to new people and experiences. As an added benefit, while I was focused on someone else's initiative, I made a connection that benefitted me.

You never know who knows who. It is important to always be approachable as well as engaging. You never know where the next introduction can lead.
I went to the focus group with no intentions of meeting someone that was good friends with an individual I was looking to meet; but that is exactly what happened. Then the person I met was willing to make an introduction which had the potential to lead to additional opportunities.

Entrepreneur

I am experiencing real life examples of how everything happens for a reason in its own divine timing. I was at a local Kroger's helping my daughter's brownie troop sell Girl Scout cookies when I saw a woman I knew from high school. At first, I said a courtesy hello without really seeing to whom I was speaking. I took a second look then realized it was Leah, a person I met in the 7th grade. Our encounter reinforced for me the need to be present acknowledging the people around me. We hugged then she asked, "what's new?" I shared how my position was eliminated in July, 2008 leading me to pursue my entrepreneurial dreams. Leah informed me that I should return the following day because Iris Cooper, a co-founder of Glory Foods as well as the Director of Ohio's Entrepreneurship & Small Business Division, would be speaking.

The next day I met Iris Cooper who was professional, approachable, and candid -- all values I respect and strive to portray. Mrs. Cooper shared her experiences detailing her entrepreneurial spirit sharing the resources available regarding how to obtain pertinent information. Hearing her speak confirmed that I was on the right path because that was the stage I was in with my venture. I felt confident and comfortable in my abilities along with the services I offered, but lacked the *how* in relation to securing clients and accessing available resources. She informed me of the Entrepreneurship event in Columbus that upcoming Monday.

I attended the Entrepreneurship seminar full of expectations and was not disappointed! I met one on one with a representative from the Dayton Small Business Development Centers/The Entrepreneur Center (SBDC/TEC) who shared her insights about my aspirations. I discovered valuable information about becoming a certified business which allowed me to position myself to conduct business with the State of Ohio. I thought the conference provided a tremendous amount of resources in one location where one could speak with subject matter experts directly. I felt that being at this conference was exactly where I needed to be at that moment in time.

The entire environment focused on celebrating entrepreneurism.

I was inspired by the words Lieutenant Governor Lee Fisher spoke as he addressed the participants. I wrote the Lieutenant Governor a letter to make him aware of my appreciation for the event. I bulleted a couple of his key items:

- Ohio will be measured by the depth of our entrepreneurial ventures, ideas and innovations
- Some of the boldest things in history happened during a crisis
- Not just survival . . . but thrival
- Wayne Gretsky skates to where the puck is going not where it is already
- What I want to be hasn't even been invented yet! Powerful statement!

I was moved by all of the speakers but my resolve was particularly strengthened by Dr. Valeriana Moeller's statement to "never waste a crisis".

This event was the springboard that I needed. I was eternally thankful to Lieutenant Governor Fisher along with his entire staff for their efforts. However, I desired to specifically acknowledge Iris and her colleague, Vanita for their support along with their commitment to entrepreneurship as well as entrepreneurial thinking. I have learned that when I benefit from an event or person, it is prudent to make my appreciation known. I made a point of acknowledging their job well done by forwarding my thoughts in writing to the appropriate individuals.

I am becoming more proficient in thinking of what will benefit others in addition to what will improve my own position. While obtaining information for my consulting firm, I also obtained information as well as contacts that would assist members of the Environmental Awareness Board of which I am an active member and the university where I facilitate as an adjunct faculty member.

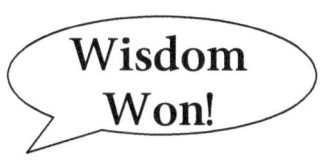

I value remaining in the moment because it enables me to acknowledge individuals around me with a warm smile and sincere hello.

I think my experience was an example of how one can be in the right place at the right time then still miss an opportunity if the focus is not on the here and now. If I would have been going through the motions by not paying attention to what was going on around me I would have missed my friend Leah and everything else that happened as a result of our *chance* meeting. Determine within yourself to be present in each moment of every day.

Being transparent allows people to connect with you in a way that leaves them wanting to know how they might be able to help your situation. People feel they can relate to a person who is candid about their circumstance. This connection could lead to the sharing of valuable information as well as contacts.

When asked "what's new?" or "how are you doing?" One could give a surface response of "oh nothing" or "I'm fine." However, providing details describing your current situation along with your desired direction allows people to see where they might assist.

When you are earnestly seeking to fulfill your passion and purpose, opportunities will find you.

Seemingly random occurrences are more destined than we realize.

Had I not encountered my high school friend, I probably would not have met Iris nor learned of the Entrepreneurial event which was tremendously helpful. I was seeking direction and I received exactly that and more even though the series of events unfolded in an unexpected manner.

Certification

I learned that there were opportunities for small business owners to be awarded business contracts with the state of Ohio. However, I was unfamiliar with the process such as where to look or who to talk with regarding legitimate means of obtaining government contracts. There are so many intermediary companies claiming to provide assistance in obtaining government contracts for a fee. However, it was difficult to decipher which companies were authentic. While I was in Columbus, Ohio for the Entrepreneurship Week, I obtained valuable information on how to become a Minority Business Enterprise (MBE) and Encouraging Diversity Growth and Equity (EDGE) certified company.

According to the Recovery.ohio.gov website the MBE certification is designed to assist minority businesses in obtaining state government contracts through a set aside procurement program for goods and services. While the EDGE certification is meant to nurture and support the growth of economically and socially underutilized businesses to foster their development and increase the number of qualified competitors in the marketplace. All of the certification terminology was new to me but the entrepreneurism conference provided an outstanding forum for me to make my inquiries real-time while receiving guidance on the spot. I used a disc from the conference titled, "How to do business with the State of Ohio" to begin my MBE/EDGE certification process.

I was informed about the Cincinnati Minority Contractor's Business Assistance Program (MCBAP) location where I met with a representative concerning my certification application prior to its submission, to ensure all of the requirements were met. I submitted my MBE/EDGE certification application obtaining feedback after a few weeks regarding information that was still required. I needed to submit my By-Laws and an Operating Agreement in addition to the other paperwork I had already submitted. The entire MBE/EDGE certification process was extremely comprehensive yet very helpful. I gained knowledge as well as relevant information regarding the documentation necessary for my business, where to find helpful templates, along with how to create a solid foundation for business operations.

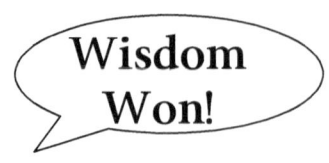

When presented with an opportunity to gain more information, take advantage even if it means traveling to another city or rearranging your schedule. That was a small price to pay for all of the information and knowledge I received while attending the Entrepreneurship Week conference.
I sought specific information about my next steps. Identify seminars or conferences offered by your state as well as local government. These forums can be valuable resources.

Don't be discouraged because a process is lengthy. The time you spend may present an opportunity to learn, grow, stretch and add to your skill sets.
I created business documents that I had never even heard of before I began this process, but now that I have completed the process I can serve as a resource for someone else.

Seeking out a mentor allowed me to learn about a whole new area of resources and services from my local Chamber of Commerce.
I did not know how vast or encompassing their assistance would be when I requested to be paired with a business mentor. The Chamber of Commerce has proven to be a tremendous support for me. Be open to new alliances; it might not be evident at the onset of how far they may take you.

Alumni

I am tremendously grateful for the generosity that Julie, from my Wednesday networking meeting, continued to extend to me. Her assistance, guidance and mentorship have been phenomenal! She probably does not realize the positive effect she has had on my life because she is just being herself. Julie shared that the upcoming Procter & Gamble (P&G) Alumni showcase would be open to the public. I registered for the event online and attended. I possessed a genuine interest in being an active collaborator to determine how I could help these business owners advance their goals while helping myself as well.

The first person I met was a gentleman that flew in from Atlanta. During our conversation, he shared contacts in Atlanta as well as Ohio that he thought might help in marketing my company. The next person I spoke with promoted wildlife and conservation. During our conversation, I explained that I was on the Environmental Awareness Board for my city of residence. Ironically, he lived the next neighborhood over from mine. When he learned that he knew members of our board, he expressed an interest in partnering opportunities. I later furnished my board with this information to determine possible next steps. He also wanted to know how I thought the involvement of minorities could be increased as it related to environmental issues. I appreciated his candor and him feeling comfortable enough with me to pose the question. We had a very engaging as well as productive conversation.

I then met an unbelievably kind individual, Scott. He stated that he had terrific mentors who never charged him for their advice. The only requirement was that he provided the same support to others. He was extremely energetic, dynamic and full of relevant information. He told me he would be willing to meet with me to assist in my endeavor because that is what others had done for him. He left me with sage words of wisdom to not give up but persist. The P&G event was a resounding success for me on a number of levels. First, I was able to connect with other business professionals identifying means of collaboration. Second, I was able to discuss my service offerings which validated my belief that I can be successful with my venture. Third, I obtained a confidence boost that just as these companies have secured clients, I can do the same. I left with valuable contacts with whom I will remain connected.

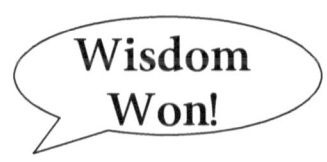

Be an active collaborator. Seek first how you can be of help to the other party. Listen intently to what they are seeking to accomplish in the short and long term future.
Offer your assistance in ways that are appropriate – volunteer, make phone calls, make an introduction, or provide honest feedback.

In spite of nervousness, put your best effort forward: smile, maintain eye contact, and ask engaging questions to overcome any anxiety you may experience.
I admit I felt a bit intimidated entering unfamiliar territory not knowing anyone. However, I knew I had to make this opportunity happen for myself; no one could do it for me. Find your voice then go for it!

Stretch beyond your comfort zone participating in activities that make you operate outside of your norm. Invite someone out for coffee if you are interested in becoming better acquainted.
You will gain strength in areas where it is needed and enhance your confidence where you are already strong. Yes, people are busy but many individuals are willing to help those who strive to help themselves. People have been where you are in life and will be glad to share their insights with a person who demonstrates a genuine interest.

BNI

Mary, from the focus group I participated in, invited me to attend a nationally recognized networking organization of which she is a member. This meeting presented an excellent opportunity to introduce my company to a new group of potential clients or contacts. Speaking to others about my business makes the entire concept more feasible in my own mind. All meeting attendees delivered a 60 second commercial about their product or service. This was a great exercise for the person presenting the commercial as well as for me on the receiving end to identify means of refining my own message. One thing I definitely wanted to incorporate was more humor in the form of a memorable tag line.

I appreciated the philosophy of the group that *givers gain.* This is a simple phrase yet so profound. The premise is to determine in what manner one can help others with their business venture then ultimately that goodwill will be reciprocated. The mindset that givers gain aligns well with what I am learning about networking on my journey of transition. There is a powerful scripture, Luke 6:38, that speaks to the rewards inherent in giving. It states,

> "Give, and it shall be given unto you; good measure, pressed down, and shaken together, and running over, shall men give into your bosom. For with the same measure that ye mete withal it shall be measured to you again.

Another strategic element I gleaned from this meeting was how comprehensive Mary was regarding the organization of her business cards. As detailed in an earlier chapter, when I obtain someone's business card I discreetly write down a memory provoking comment. This method has been helpful when I meet people for lunch to have a genuine point of interest to discuss. Not only did Mary organize her cards in a visible portfolio she demonstrated her active interest in sharing contacts while assisting others network when there was a good connection. She strategically maintained 3 to 4 business cards of each person she meets so that she can help them network by handing out their cards when appropriate. She inspired me to the point that I acquired my own business card portfolio to assist in building relationships.

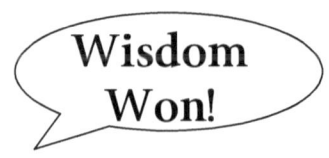

It is smart to learn from others to discover what methods are effective when creating your own style of conveying who you are and what you have to offer.

You always want to retain your originality; however, there is nothing new under the sun so there is no need to recreate the wheel. What makes you unique is the way in which you combine resources and ideas to make them your own.

Humor is powerful in breaking the ice going a long way in helping people relate to one another. Select a memorable phrase that emulates the nature of your product or service when promoting yourself or business.

Generate a descriptive slogan letting the creative juices flow. Spend some quiet time with a pen and pad to capture the concepts you create. Infuse humor where appropriate not taking yourself too seriously.

Have an organized approach to following up with the people you meet along with seeking opportunities to connect others.

When I saw Mary give a card to someone that she thought would be a good connection for them, even though the party represented by the card was not there, that influenced me to want to do the same. It is very kind as well as professional to make connections on someone else's behalf.

Authentic

For as long as I can remember I endured an internal conflict between my beliefs and actions. I did not feel authentic but did not know how to make a change. Although I have always been blessed with what would be considered good jobs, great career opportunities, along with commensurate salaries; there was always something missing. When I had a bad day at work, I would write down what I would be doing if money were no issue. Over the years, I have kept these lists eventually putting them in a folder to revisit one day. At the beginning of my job transition, I reviewed that file finding the earliest note was dated 1997 equating to over 10 years of thoughts and ideas. Amazingly common themes surfaced that remained relatively consistent throughout the years.

Having this information at my disposal allowed me to focus my efforts on my true talents as well as God given abilities. There were quite a few things I was capable of doing but what was my passion and purpose? This process of self-discovery helped me realize I needed to focus on fulfilling my purpose. I've heard the question stated, "What would you do if you had millions of dollars with money not being an issue?" Even with that desirable scenario, I could not clearly pinpoint what I desired to achieve in my life. I could discern talent and potential in other people; however, it was difficult to identify the same within myself. I began contemplating my life experiences thinking what can I share with others from my heart because I lived it? Obstacles I personally endured eventually overcoming included low self-esteem along with a lack of self-confidence. I began to determine that I could assist young girls who felt as I did growing up, overcome undesirable circumstances.

My familiarity with the topic of vision, along with reading about the subject, instilled in me the importance of establishing a clear vision for your life. Children are encouraged to cultivate a mindset that they can accomplish anything. However, if they do not have someone in their life to help them gain an appreciation for their innate talents and skills it will be difficult to achieve their full potential. I desire to inspire young people by helping them instill confidence within themselves that they can be successful. The example I strive to provide is for youth to put God first as well as be true to themselves while valuing the attributes of others.

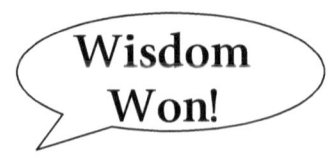

Wisdom Won!

If you encounter an internal gnawing, don't ignore it. Explore it. Identify the root cause as well as source of the discontent. First and foremost, you need to be true to yourself.

What common themes are in your heart month after month, year after year? Begin working towards fulfilling those passions.

A worthwhile goal is to be whole: spirit, mind and body without denying any part of your person. Think about your own personal experiences identifying what you have survived that will encourage someone else.

What information, knowledge, and wisdom can you impart? Even poor judgment resulting in bad choices can be immensely valuable in demonstrating what to avoid. Allow your mess to be transformed into your message of inspiration for others dealing with similar issues.

Observe those around you providing them with feedback on what they do well, particularly children. Be creative in empowering others such as writing a note to your friend's children making them aware of the positive characteristics you observe.

At times, we think something good about a person but never verbalize our positive impression. I believe perhaps we think the person is already aware of the specific strength we see in them. This may or may not be true. Your positive feedback may improve someone's day or go as far as altering the trajectory of a child's life.

Legacy

As I waited in the car line to pick up my children from school, I began to reflect on my position being eliminated resulting in me going from a successful executive to being unemployed in a matter of hours. One of my initial thoughts was my children considering how this would alter their lives. Our children attended private school, therefore, an immediate question was, "how will we continue to pay tuition?" Within days of being notified about my job elimination, I spoke with the Head of School sharing the recent developments. I desired for our children to remain in familiar surroundings therefore I sought assistance to make that feasible. The Head of School made arrangements that assisted us in keeping our children at their school.

Our situation highlighted the need for support to those who sustain an unexpected circumstance. Tax returns normally provide the basis for many forms of assistance. While I understand this method results in a uniform as well as standard basis it sometimes inaccurately portrays a person's current financial standing. We were in a position where our prior year tax returns indicated that we made too much money for certain assistance when the reality was my income was zero. I decided that when I was in a position to do so I would establish a fund for individuals who appeared stable on paper but in reality needed interim support.

So as I sat in the car on this particular day, I recounted the events that transpired over the last few months considering how much had changed. During that time period, I re-launched and re-branded my consulting firm along with attending the Entrepreneurship Week in Columbus Ohio. I had become acutely aware of the importance of entrepreneurism and entrepreneurial thinking. In that moment, my interim support idea evolved into an entrepreneurial focus that in addition to providing financial assistance would foster entrepreneurial thinking. My desire was to begin a fund offering interim financial support that focused on entrepreneurial thinking.

Then my thoughts switched to what should the fund be titled? Should we use our children's name? Should we use my husband's name along with my own? Then I was struck by the inspiration to name the fund after my grandparents who were entrepreneurial in nature in how they cultivated their own gardens, created inventions, built additions to their home, opened a tool sharpening business as well as being a masterful cook and gifted seamstress. They provided an example of overcoming difficulties while proactively making things occur instead of waiting for them to happen. My grandparents provided the perfect link between my past and future. That is how the Ernest and Annie Cameron Sr. Entrepreneur Foundation came into existence.

    I was really excited about the creation of this fund; however, I also wanted to pay tribute to my paternal grandparents. My other passion was for people to have vision in fulfilling their purpose. My paternal grandfather passed away possibly without realizing his full potential or seeing his legacy fulfilled. I viewed this as a full circle moment where his life can serve as a testament to others. Ultimately his life will be the catalyst to assist countless people secure vision and fulfill their purpose. I initiated The

Lauren and Katherine Brown Sr. Vision & Purpose Foundation to honor their contributions.

I shared my plans to establish the aforementioned foundations with my friend Scott, he generously told me to consider him a partner. On a different occasion, I had lunch with my friend Marie where I informed her about the foundation; she stated that she and her husband wanted to be involved even to the point of providing financial support. I began researching the mechanics of structuring a public foundation on the Internal Revenue Service (IRS) website. There were more requirements than I imagined; however, I welcome the challenge.

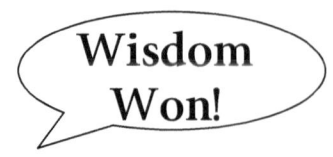

As much as feasible, complete tasks when they come to mind instead of procrastinating. I strive to contact people when I think of them versus stating that I had good intentions but never got around to it.

I think a large component of leaving a legacy is letting people know how meaningful they are to you; conveying the impact they made on your life while they are here to appreciate the acknowledgment.

Bridge the gap between the past and the future. There is an abundance of wisdom that can be gained from our elders. While advances in technology are phenomenal, nothing can compare to an afternoon chat with an elder in your family or neighborhood.

Emulate the grace and dignity with which many of our ancestors operate. There is something to be said for being resourceful, respectful and honorable. Many of the admirable characteristics we attain are attributable to the elders we are fortunate to interact with on a regular basis.

Celebrate all aspects of yourself even if there are characteristics that are not currently desirable. We are all a work in progress. If there are attributes within your personality that you acquired from familial traits, assess whether they should be nurtured or changed.

If you find yourself adopting negative family traits, reclaim your power thereby changing your life as well as the legacy for future generations. You can be the catalyst overcoming adverse aspects of your family's past turning what could be considered a negative into a favorable outcome for future generations.

Fitness

Although I have been fortunate to maintain a small body stature over the years, I knew I needed to improve my cardiovascular strength. My husband is frugal when it comes to spending, so when he told me he wanted to purchase the P90X workout program I knew he would be committed. I demonstrated my excitement about him wanting to improve his health by committing to workout with him. Primarily, I viewed my participation solely as bolstering my husband's efforts; however, I quickly discovered that the P90X workout would be beneficial for me as well. When we received the DVD's, we completed the initial assessment of performing jumping jacks for two minutes. Jumping jacks for two minutes that would be a breeze, or so I thought! This initial Fit Test showed me just how much I was out of shape! Those two minutes seemed like an eternity; I couldn't believe my lack of stamina!

My husband and I exercising jointly revealed that the two of us had not engaged in a common goal or hobby in a long time. It felt great doing something good for ourselves, and accomplishing it together while encouraging each other. This experience showed me that we need to proactively seek out activities to achieve together. We engage in couple activities such as going to the movies along with spending time with our friends. However, we had not participated in a common as well as focused purpose in a while. Our mutual focus on physical fitness brought us together in a special way. A peripheral benefit to our exercising is that it increased our stamina in *every* area of our lives, if you know what I mean!

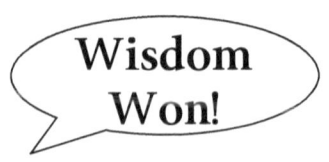

Taking care of yourself physically is important to your overall well being. I know this aspect of life gets lost in the shuffle sometimes; however, strive to ensure exercise remains a priority.

A well portioned diet or food regimen is essential in achieving balance in your life while maintaining your health. Work to infuse your diet with fresh fruits and vegetables.

Being alongside your "someone special" is a wonderful means to enhance closeness whether it involves taking in a movie, going to a play or snuggling up on the couch.

That togetherness is deepened when working to achieve a common goal. Assess whether you and your loved ones, particularly your significant other are engaging in activities together.

Exercise is demanding; requiring discipline, focus and consistency. It can be strenuous; however, over a period of time results are evident providing the much needed encouragement to continue.

Sometimes the boost you receive from something as simple as completing additional repetitions is tremendous. Building on your prior success can result in greater endurance, feeling stronger, along with acquiring more energy. Obtain clearance from your doctor, find the right program for you then get moving!

Impactful

During my period of transition, various avenues have opened for me personally, professionally and spiritually as I seek to fulfill my purpose. Dr. Cindy Trimm was instrumental in my transformation. I included excerpts from Dr. Cindy Trimm's scripturally based words of wisdom; some of which are included in her outstanding books "Commanding Your Morning" and "The Rules of Engagement". She expounded on the tools required for a person to successfully navigate the road to prosperity including the ability to operate with integrity, live authentically, live impeccably, along with being credible.

One of the profound points she made was how rejection becomes your gift. I realize this is not the perspective many people would normally take about being rejected. However, her statement resonated with me making tremendous sense. Her explanation was that sometimes when people reject you, it is not because you are inferior, but superior, leaving others without the capacity to handle you. Rejection is at times an outward reflection of a person's inward insecurities. Dr. Trimm equated rejection to a sign that one was not going to prosper in their current space or with a particular person, but were meant to move forward to their place of prosperity.

She also spoke on the importance of prayer focusing on how prayer shifts climates as well as atmospheres. The book, "Understanding the Purpose and Power of Prayer" by Dr. Myles Munroe is one of the best resources I have read to supplement my understanding of prayer. This book provided me with a better comprehension of effective prayer. I learned the importance of praying God's Word when I pray instead of solely using my own thoughts. For example, when I pray for direction I speak Proverbs 3:5-6 as a basis for my faith. Jesus himself used the Word of God as basis for addressing situations. When Jesus was being attacked by Satan he told him, "It is written, Man shall not live by bread alone, but by every word that proceedeth out of the mouth of God" (Matthew 4:4). I have found it beneficial to emulate the methods that Jesus used and appreciate resources that align with His example.

Dr. Myles Munroe taught on Leadership and Crisis during a conference I attended. He expounded on how your gift makes room for you. He indicated that true leaders never seek leadership; they simply become their true selves. He reflected on how Jesus informed us that we would have trouble in our lives based on John 16:33 - 17:1. Dr. Munroe stated that some individual's faith is not built for adversity. A strong foundation of faith means believing in God no matter what! People tend to lose their faith if they are not healed or lose their house or experience a difficult situation where they feel their prayer went unanswered.

For example, in the Bible when Daniel was facing the Lion's Den (Daniel chapter 6), and the three men faced the fiery furnace (Daniel chapter 3) I can imagine them praying that God save them from their respective adversities. In Daniel 3:17 the three men believed for God to deliver them from the burning fiery furnace. However, God saw fit not to deliver them from their circumstance, in the manner they probably imagined, but provided grace and protection as they endured it. I am finding the same is true today. Sometimes we believe and pray to be delivered from a situation; however, God sees fit to not remove the circumstance but allow us to endure it to build our faith while glorifying Him. Dr. Munroe expounded on the fact that to successfully navigate life, one must expect change. Sometimes depression and disappointment result from the mindset that circumstances will never change remaining status quo.

Dr. Munroe stated God, who can handle trouble, desires his children to be strong in dealing with problems also. Crisis comes to expose as well as test maturity. Not all change is an improvement; however, without change there can be no improvement. Dr. Munroe spoke about how true leaders plan change by initiating it, anticipating it then managing it, not by panicking. He stated leaders are tested in bad times, providing proof about their character. True leadership uses change as well as crisis for growth and development. Crisis produces sharp leaders while refining them. Crossroads can be viewed as the incubator of creativity, new concepts, and the pressure that forces innovation. Shakespeare who is viewed as one of the greatest writers of all time used the following phrase in one of his plays,

"Sweet are the uses of adversity . . . "

This combination of words may appear contradictory; however, when you are facing difficult times your mind is usually at its sharpest allowing you to think as well as behave differently using dilemmas to your benefit.

It has been said there is nothing new under the sun. Dr. Munroe provided insight on this saying. He explained how new really means innovation. In reality every idea, product or service considered "new" is a combination of old things. Sometimes when crisis occurs it forces us to look at old things in new combinations. Dr. Munroe provided some powerful examples, such as:

>new sweater = old lamb's wool,
>new suit = old silk, and
>new house = old dirt

He posed a very profound question. Could Moses have built an aircraft? After a moment of silence Dr. Munroe explained that everything necessary to build an aircraft was present on earth when Moses was alive. However, the knowledge required to put pieces in the correct combination was not evident at that time. This was a very interesting concept to me that everything we need is at our disposal; however, we must identify the correct combinations for our particular situations.

Dr. Munroe shared an encounter he had with an unemployed woman. He proposed that she stop crying, gain her composure and consider how her gift could sustain her family. He made a distinction between a person's job and their gift. He told her she had lost her job but not her gift. Knowing something about the woman, he suggested she explore her talent of baking cookies. He recommended that she allow individuals to sample them first and then once she gained a following to begin selling them. She was more financially stable after her job loss than she had been with her previous employer.

Dr. Munroe also taught that no one succeeds without the following three principles I am obligated, I am eager and I am not ashamed based on the Bible teaching in Romans 1:14-16. He conveyed that you cannot truly become a leader until you discover your obligation to humanity. Dr. Munroe indicated that leaders are born when they discover what they *must* do. Being eager results from discovering your passion, working within your passion motivates you. Dr. Munroe described passion as a zeal within you that if everybody abandons you, you will continue on your own. When you find that type of drive, you have identified your obligation. I gave a monetary donation on Thursday of the conference. The following day I received a call regarding an adjunct professor opportunity which would provide our family with another stream of income! I have experienced firsthand that when you give, you definitely receive!

Wisdom Won!

Operating with integrity while living your life authentically are cornerstones to a successful and fulfilled life.
There are people that appear to be successful but are really empty shells without fulfillment. Build your success the correct way by utilizing strong principles so that you can enjoy the fruit of your labor.

Put rejection in perspective. Rejection has been a bigger driver in my life than I realized. I experienced rejection when I was younger as well as in adulthood. I took the feeling of being disregarded personally; internalizing it to the point that I was unwilling to accept myself.
However, I have grown in the area of self-acceptance. Through her teaching, Cyndi Trimm helped confirmed for me how rejection should be viewed. Learn to accept yourself to the point that you move away from situations or people where you are being tolerated instead of valued. You are worthy of better treatment.

Many individuals have found themselves in a crisis; particularly in our current economic times. I began evaluating my gifts to determine what I could combine in a different way that I had not considered previously.
I found that I have been more creative as well as resourceful out of necessity. I directly attribute

growth in certain areas of my life to being in a situation that stretched me as a person.

How

I feel that God has provided me with insights on my purpose along with what He would have me do with my life. Now I am at a place of *how* do I achieve my goals? So many wonderful resources, people and information have crossed my path serving as stepping stones to my next phase in life. It is becoming my default that when doors of opportunity open, I stride through them without hesitation. Openings present themselves in various ways. A breakthrough may not always be as clear cut as winning a coveted meeting with a potential client. It could come in the form of attending a free seminar on entrepreneurism sponsored by your city that is ripe with networking occasions.

I have found that when I share what I am looking to do, people are eager to help me with information, contacts and potential clients. When I receive helpful information I share it with everyone I know in case they are interested or know someone that may benefit.

My mindset has shifted to consciously take others into consideration. If a recruiter sends me a job posting that is not a fit for my background, I forward it to others who might be interested.

While I had lunch with a family friend, a person that we mutually knew stopped by to say hello. This individual asked me to forward his contact information on to a friend of his that I knew. It is critically important to follow through on commitments in an immediate fashion. I e-mailed the person who stopped by our table to say hello expressing that it was great to see him at lunch as well as informing him that I passed on his contact information as promised. Approximately one week later, I received an e-mail from the person I had seen at lunch saying he viewed my website and thought he could utilize my consulting services. We scheduled an initial consultation for the following week.

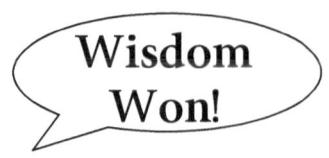

The "how" behind achieving my goals relates to spending quiet time each day to determine what I desire to happen then I visualize my plans unfolding.

I listen for divine inspiration in the form of ideas, thoughts and next steps. I take one step at a time towards achieving what I know for certain then continue to seek guidance for the rest.

Seek out resources and information that are applicable to you from your local government. There are untapped programs and opportunities that could be beneficial to what you desire to achieve.

Attend council meetings to understand the priorities of your city identifying how you can be involved in facilitating positive change. This will net you exposure with city officials while enhancing your understanding of what initiatives could impact you as a resident.

I attribute the interest expressed in my consulting service being a direct result of my prompt follow-up in an unrelated matter in addition to their being a current need.

How you operate in everyday life serves as a reflection of how you will operate in other arenas. Whether that is an accurate assessment or not, your behavior helps to form other people's perceptions. Ensure you are consistent in everything you do.

Paradigm

When I attended a P&G Alumni function I met some dynamic people; one of them being Scott, the CEO of his own communications firm. What I have discovered about networking is that it is important to interact with everyone that you can at an event; even though it may only result in a few lasting connections. The important aspect is the quality of the relationships being built. I followed up with Scott inviting him to meet for lunch. We discussed how success equates to personal growth. We engaged in a thought provoking discussion with Scott posing poignant questions. I really appreciated the interest he demonstrated by probing to know more about what I desired to achieve. He was the sounding board I needed because I did not have anyone to speak to about my entrepreneurial pursuits. Scott was able to share with me his rich experiences gained through his own entrepreneurial pursuits. He challenged me to test my paradigms that were reflected in my typical pattern of thinking and behaving.

I told him I have always had an entrepreneurial mindset but never seemed to have the time to pursue my own venture with balancing a full time job as well as family commitments. However, when my position was eliminated in July, 2008, I felt as if God was providing the time I said I needed. As I shared with Scott the details about my consulting business he asked excellent questions such as, "what is my endpoint?" "why was I embarking on this business?" "what would I do if I had the financial independence I spoke about so fondly?"

Once we began talking more in depth I told him if I were financially independent I would write, speak, and present empowerment forums to equip youth with necessary life skills. He asked me why I was not doing that now; what was my delay? My response related to needing additional monies to fund my initiatives. Interestingly enough, I could see where I was still employing my "I will fulfill my dream *one day*" approach even though I was operating my own consulting firm. Although I was leading my own firm, I was still using it as an interim step deferring what I truly desired to be achieving.

How could I position myself to fulfill my passion instead of falling back into my safety net of what I know I am capable of achieving? Scott made me realize that even with my own company, I had not truly reached my ultimate goal and was not really moving in that direction. I was still on an interim step to my true purpose. Not that there is anything wrong with interim steps, it is just that they should be recognized as such.

Scott displayed tremendous generosity by offering me office space at no cost equipped with a conference room along with an administrative assistant to add more polish to my operations when dealing with clients. He was willing to provide these accommodations for me simply because his mentor did similar things for him. I told him I was extremely appreciative. I would contemplate his offer then let him know if I were ready to take that next step. Once our lunch concluded, I thought more and more about ways to make my writing a priority in my life. How would I translate my passion into earnings? I knew I should do what I love then the money would follow, but how do I realistically navigate that mindset when I have financial obligations? Just as I was pondering all of this thinking that I needed some clarity, I checked my voicemail and saw that I had a message.

The message was from Edward, a man that I attended high school with and recently reconnected with on LinkedIn.com. He called me to learn more about my business. I returned his call realizing as we spoke we had many attributes in common. We both attended the same university after high school, we started businesses within 1 year of each other and we both had an entrepreneurial mindset. We had a meaningful conversation. It was refreshing speaking to someone that was likeminded accomplishing goals I am looking to achieve.

He was generous with his contacts telling me to view his LinkedIn profile, identify who I would be interested in conducting business with and he would be willing to make the introductions. I appreciated his offer because I am at the stage of building my client base; therefore solid introductions were exactly what I needed. When I inquired about Ed's initiatives so that I could help promote his efforts he told me to focus on being successful then he could tell people he knows me I was impressed with his response. Talking with Edward gave me clarity that I needed to continue with my business venture as well as other projects.

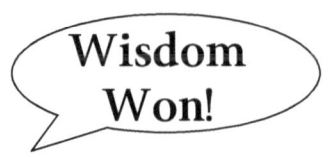

It is alright that everyone you meet will not be a permanent contact. Certain connections are for a season in your life.
If you reach out to someone and you can tell that there is not going to be an active relationship, make sure you maintain their information to determine if there is a helpful connection you can help them facilitate.

Scott challenged my thinking on why I was not currently doing what I felt was my passion but still operating at an interim step. That was an excellent question. My practical response was I needed to generate assets; but in my heart I knew he was right.
It has been said do what you love and the money will follow. I believed in that sentiment; however my actions did not consistently reflect my belief. My financial commitments did not have to keep me from moving forward with my passion. I made a conscious decision to be deliberate in my efforts to attain balance in accomplishing something in line with my passion daily.

Social networking websites such as LinkedIn are extremely powerful. These platforms are beneficial tools to assist in building as well as maintaining relationships.
Connect with past or new contacts through reputable social networks. This interaction affords you the

opportunity to describe your initiatives while assessing how to support the efforts of people within your network. Consider utilizing the recommendation function in LinkedIn to endorse the positive attributes others have demonstrated.

Timing

I was in the midst of filling my car with gas when a nicely dressed gentleman exited his car. I commented that he was wearing a nice hat as he walked into the store; he smiled. When he came out of the store he said hello; I introduced myself then he told me his name. Ironically, we discovered our children attended the same school along with the fact we both taught at the same university. This encounter reinforced the need to be personable not shut up in your own world. Otherwise, impromptu meetings could pass without notice.

When I arrived home, I discovered the individual I met at the filling station had sent me a LinkedIn invitation. Earlier that day I was looking at a list of acquaintance's e-mails. Ironically, I saw the person's name that I ended up meeting later in the day. I knew him in passing but would not have e-mailed him the business opportunity I was disseminating since we had not formally met. Then that same afternoon, I met him in person at the gas station!

Another example of timing that I am grateful for related to our taxes. On April 15, I paid our taxes to the State of Ohio which ended up being significant because I received unemployment without taxes being deducted. I filed our local taxes about two weeks prior which resulted in a refund. That amount would thankfully help offset the State of Ohio taxes that were due. However, when I filed the local taxes I was told the municipality had up to 90 days to issue a refund check. Therefore I was not expecting our refund anytime soon. To my surprise, when I opened our mailbox on April 15, our local tax refund was enclosed! I had just filed the Ohio taxes that morning with the offset funds arriving that afternoon! The timing of these events perfectly met our exact needs!

Timing is everything. Maximize being in the right place at the right time. Many times you optimize opportunities by being aware of your surroundings living consciously, not in a fog.
When I am in tune with myself as well as those around me, I can perceive when I should move versus when I should stay still, or when I should speak instead of being silent. Discerning what is occurring around you will enable you to attract the right opportunities.

Giving a genuine compliment can open the door to meaningful conversation. Work to create a balance between being cautious with placing yourself in a position to meet a new contact.
I could have averted my eyes to avoid eye contact or not said anything to the gentleman at the gas station, causing that entire scenario to play out differently. Sometimes what are considered "chance" encounters are heavily influenced by our own willingness to extend ourselves to other people.

Be appreciative when things work in your favor. Don't dismiss a good turn of events as being immaterial. Instead display an attitude of gratitude. Maintain a positive demeanor along with a thankful attitude; these attributes will take you far in life.
I have witnessed where my positive attitude appears to work as a magnet to attract positive people and

situations to me while repelling negative individuals and circumstances.

Creative

I contacted the Executive Recruiter who assisted me in obtaining my previous job. I inquired if he would inform me of contractor opportunities where companies needed someone with my background and experience but did not want to commit to a full-time salary with benefits. I also reached out to a search firm I had never worked with, but thought it would be good to become affiliated with them. This search firm had a job posting for a Senior Audit Manager where a couple of the qualifications required did not align with my background; however, I thought I would contact the placement service anyway. I admit I was a little nervous calling Chris, the contact person who was also the President of the search firm.

I expressed that I was interested in exploring contract opportunities between my consulting firm and his clients. I received Chris' voicemail; however, he returned my call in a short amount of time. We spoke on a Friday resulting in me forwarding my resume to him. We had a breakfast meeting that following Tuesday. Calling Chris was a calculated risk that for some people would be no big deal, but for others the possible rejection would have been too much to handle. Chris turned out to be extremely professional providing me with very good insights. He showed a genuine interest in assisting me by suggesting that I compile an Executive Summary to serve as an addendum to my resume when he marketed my abilities to his clients. On Wednesday of that same week, Chris called me with a referral to a client with rapid growth who was possibly in need of assistance with their internal control structure. I researched the company then contacted the owner to determine how our services could be of assistance.

Opportunities do not have to be a perfect match for you to pursue it. Sometimes people are seeking an ideal candidate but will be interested in talking with a person who possesses the majority of the necessary qualifications.

Even though all of my qualifications did not align with a specific opportunity; I could at least pursue contracting possibilities. You never know unless you ask.

Usually situations turn out better than anticipated. While the initial focus was Chris helping me, there could be ways that I could assist him as well by sharing contacts as well as relevant information.

Many scenarios can ultimately be mutually beneficial if you are willing to be proactive, creative and open to taking a calculated risk.

When you inform other people about a direction you would like to take, they will keep you in mind assessing how they can assist you in attaining your goals.

When Chris next spoke to his client, he proactively inquired about their control structure specifically thinking of how I might assist them. Our interaction was reciprocal in nature because whenever I came across a candidate looking for a company or company looking for a great candidate, I would recommend Chris as a liaison.

Coincidence

My children were on Spring Break so I tried to identify fun activities that were inexpensive as well as indoors since the weather was cool and rainy. For Wednesday of that week, I thought skating would be fun; however, the open skate did not begin until 6pm. This time did not fit into our plans because I wanted to have an activity that occurred during the day. In addition, I was facilitating a class that evening. Therefore, remaining flexible, I moved on to an alternate plan. I initially planned to take my children to the movies on Thursday, so I switched the movies to Wednesday and skating until Thursday when open skate was earlier in the day.

On Thursday while my children were skating, I was reading for class when a woman made a nice comment as she walked past me. I want to reiterate the importance of being approachable and friendly. I can't recall exactly what she said, but I took note of demeanor and smiled at her. Then later she came over to where I was sitting to ask if she could give me one of her business cards. I told her sure turning my attention from what I was reading to inquire about her work. I have discovered it is important to focus on the initiatives and dreams of others to help bring about your own - that is true networking. I am learning how to truly engage by listening intently to determine how I or someone I know may be of help.

As Tia shared her business concept with obvious passion, the thought came to mind that my mom was involved in an initiative that might complement what she was doing. I knew my mom would not mind me connecting her with someone with a similar vision. While giving Tia my mom's cell phone number I told her my mom's name is Sharon but most people know her as Diane. She exclaimed, "Diane is your mother? I know Diane!" Come to find out my mother used to work with Tia's husband.

So then she says she needs someone that can help her with completing her DVD for her Workbook Project. I told her that I know a man named Rick who enjoys production projects. So I called Rick to see if it was alright for me to connect him with Tia and he said sure. As a result of their conversation, they discovered they had similar projects in process. This created an opportunity for them to mutually benefit from each other's experience. This connection occurred because one individual was willing to interact with a person who was a stranger but later became a new contact. This encounter could have transpired completely different. She could have decided not to approach me even though she felt strongly that she should talk to me. I could have said no thank you to her card, or I could have taken her card then returned to what I was doing instead of engaging her in further conversation. This is an example of how much of a difference a few kind words along with genuine interest can make!

I believe people cross your path at the appointed time. Tia and I seemed destined to meet. This is a common theme throughout this book; but it is so important to be approachable taking an interest in the people around you.

A smile along with eye contact can go a long way. Try demonstrating how approachable you are on a consistent basis if you are not already.

Even if the person you meet shares something that is not of direct interest to you, consider who in your circle may benefit or might be a resource for that person.

Instead of mentally checking out of the conversation if you think your interests do not align; think of someone else who might be a resource.

When you meet someone, take a few minutes to really understand their current work along with what they desire to accomplish long term.

Ask appropriate questions to gain an understanding as well as express your interest. You never know who knows who and what beneficial relationships can be established.

Choices

In a quiet moment of thought, a particular television program popped into my mind. I thought... wow... that's one of my favorite shows. It would come on as a marathon and I would watch one episode after another. I heard a thought in my head, just as clear, stating that even though this was one of my favorite programs, it was not good for me to watch it. I had a choice to make.

I spent almost two days filling out a job application only to find out that only internal candidates were being considered. On top of that, my car was hit while I was pulling out of the parking lot where I hand delivered my application. It was a blessing that the driver admitted fault along with having car insurance. It's not a huge deal, but I inquired about what car I would receive for my rental. When the representative specified the possible models, I considered them subcompact cars. Granted, I don't need a lot of space but I would like to have a comfortable vehicle. When I talked to my insurance company, they informed me that I could have any car I wanted as long as I paid the difference on the daily rate. I did not want to incur an additional cost, so I relinquished the situation with peace.

When the rental agent pulled into the repair shop parking lot, he was driving a subcompact. I thought to myself, "that is fine; all things are working together for my good." I entered the car with a good attitude having a great conversation with the rental agent on the way back to the rental location. Once we arrived inside the rental location, I was preparing to sign my paperwork when he asked did I want to keep the car he picked me up in or did I want to drive the red 2009 SUV they had parked out front. I told him I would like the SUV thanking him for the option. I don't know this for certain but I attributed him suggesting the SUV because of my positive attitude. If I would have chosen to have a negative disposition because of the car I had initially been given, I could have missed out on a blessing. When I surrendered the situation, it worked out for my good in a way that was better than what I would have even asked.

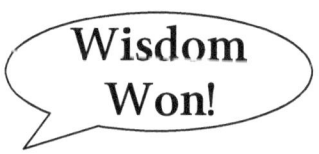

I am more focused on the fact that I have a choice in every situation I find myself in and am keenly aware of the consequences of the choices I decide to make.

There are times external forces are at work resulting in our being in a particular situation; however, I have found that sometimes outcomes in our lives are a direct result of our personal choices.

God provides us the choice to do things according to His Will or not. It might not be a life altering choice that he asks us to make. At times, it is not even so much a right or wrong choice; it's just not the choice for you.

The consequence of not making the appropriate choice for you might not be obvious or immediate. However, it is prudent to remain obedient and in line with God's will for our lives.

We can choose to have an attitude of gratitude instead of an unpleasant disposition. Seeing the good in even the smallest of situations can position you to receive unexpected benefits.

While I could fixate on what I think is not going right in my life, I have learned that what I focus on influences my thoughts and ultimately my behaviors. When I behave in a friendly manner I tend to receive that treatment in return.

Finale

I feel that this book is now complete. The origins were my personal experiences in being unemployed during difficult economic times and the lessons I learned along the way that seemed that they would be helpful to others as well. I have learned through my journey of transition that what I experience is bigger than me and can be shared for the greater good.

So I do consider this a record of what I have experienced as well as insight into my life as a person just like you who has dealt with adversity and are still here to tell about it. In many ways, I am better for having gone through it. I have learned that I am *full of it!*

My business, Activate Consulting, is established and I am now even certified to do business with my state. I am continuing my adjunct professor work as well as working on other writing projects; look for those in the near future.

I am living the life that I want to live. I have the flexibility and balance in my life that I have desired for a long time. I am able to spend quality time with my husband, my children, my family and friends. I've put the wisdom that I won to use and it has benefitted me tremendously.

I hope this serves as an encouragement to you that if it happened for me, it can happen for you too! Remember . . . You're Full of It!

The Author of . . .

YOU'RE **FULL** OF IT!

Is a dynamic speaker who captivates her audience by employing interactive techniques.

Authentic and engaging, she employs practical methods to empower others to maximize their inner strength.

To have Chandra inspire your group or organization by telling them what they're *full of,* contact us at yourefullofit.net!

www.ingramcontent.com/pod-product-compliance
Lightning Source LLC
LaVergne TN
LVHW051551070426
835507LV00021B/2527